March, 2003

The

HANDBOOK

JOHN GAUNTNER

TUTTLE PUBLISHING
Boston • Rutland, Vermont • Tokyo

First published in 2002 by Tuttle Publishing, an imprint of Periplus Editions (HK) Ltd., with editorial offices at 153 Milk Street, Boston, Massachusetts 02109.

Library of Congress Cataloging-in-Publication Data

Gauntner, John.
The saké handbook / John Gauntner, — Rev. ed.
    p. cm.
Includes index.
ISBN 0-8048-3425-3
1. Rice wines. I. Title.

TP579 .G38 2002
641.2'3–dc21

2002067291

Distributed by

North America, Latin America, & Europe
Tuttle Publishing
Distribution Center
Airport Industrial Park
364 North Clarendon, VT
05759-9436
Tel: (802) 773-8930
Fax: (802) 773-6993

Asia Pacific
Berkeley Books Pte. Ltd.
130 Joo Seng Road
#06-01/03 Olivine Building
Singapore 368357
Tel: (65) 6280-1330
Fax: (65) 6280-6290

Japan & Korea
Tuttle Publishing
Yaekari Building, 3F
5-4-2 Ōsaki
Shinagawa-ku
Tokyo 141 0032
Tel: 81-35-437-0701
Fax: 81-35-437-0755

Second Edition
05 04 03 02   9 8 7 6 5 4 3 2 1

Design by Barbara Poeter, Castelton, VT
Printed in the United States of America

CONTENTS

A *sugidama*, or large ball of tightly bundled cedar, hangs from the roof of this sakagura. Also known as a *sakabayashi*, it is perhaps the most traditional way of marking a place where saké can be found.

INTRODUCTION

THE DEPTH OF the saké world in Japan is overwhelming. Trying to learn about it from square one can be a bit intimidating, to say the least. A good saké shop is often stocked with hundreds of different labels with seemingly unreadable names and bearing descriptions that most shoppers feel they cannot understand without excessive research. Going to a saké pub or a decent *izakaya*, a traditional Japanese pub-style restaurant, can be even worse, as carefully selected saké are listed in artistic calligraphy, further inhibiting the reading efforts of the uninitiated.

This wall comes tumbling down rather quickly though, since the terminology can be learned fairly quickly, and remembering the names and styles of just a few saké can take you a long way. Knowing just a little bit has a way of bringing you into situations and in touch with people that teach you just a little bit more, or introduce you to just one more wonderful saké.

The first part of this book gets down to the nitty-gritty. Just how is the stuff made anyway? What's the big deal? What kind of eccentric people actually ferment rice? How hard is it to make the stuff? What steps are involved? A somewhat detailed explanation of the process is given in what is (hopefully) a relatively clear presentation.

Strange terminology flies around the saké world like leaves in the autumn wind. Most of it has origins in the actual brewing process, and is difficult to decipher even for native Japanese speakers. But once you have a grip on it, things are fairly straightforward. Here, as comprehensive a lexicon as possible has been presented in a simple and easy-to-use format.

The trick is to begin to find your own likes and dislikes, and to develop a discerning palate. Linguistic barriers collapse when interest is strong, and it can be amazing what you remember when you like something.

What I have written is precisely the type of book I wish I had possessed when I arrived in Japan: a concise, detailed, and user-friendly guide to the world of saké. This book does not dwell upon the historical and social significance of saké; rather, it is a book that tells you what's out there, where to buy it, and where to drink it. It's meant to be something you can stuff in your pocket and refer to in front of the saké shelf at the store, or open at a restaurant and use to double check a saké listed on the menu. It's meant to be a book that makes things linguistically transparent, or at least translucent, so that the reader can begin to develop his or her own appreciation for saké that is as deep and educated as any expert's.

PART ONE

その一
酒造の話

CHAPTER ONE

HOW SAKÉ IS MADE

*S*aké — though long shrouded in misconception, veiled by language, and isolated by island geography — is one of the most refined, interesting, and enjoyable beverages in the world. In its finer manifestations, it is as fascinating in flavor, fragrance, and history as any wine, spirit, or beer. But before getting into that, it is important to address the question of just what saké is, and how it is made.

Chances are, if you are reading this book, you have a good understanding of how some alcoholic beverages are produced. When it comes to saké, it is often labeled as a wine, due to the lack of carbonation and relatively high alcohol content (15 to 20 percent), or as a beer, since it is made with grain (rice) and not fruit. In actuality, saké making differs enough from both the wine- and beer-making processes to justify a category all its own.

A quick look at how these three beverages are made should clear things up a bit.

Wine is a fermented beverage. Fermentation is the process by which yeast converts sugar to alcohol and carbon dioxide, which, in the case of wine, is allowed to escape. Sugars are already present in the grape juice, and these sugars are ready for use by the yeast cells as food and nutrients. Although this simple and short explanation does not do justice to the age-old art of wine making, it will serve our purposes here.

Beer calls for another step in the process. There is no fermentable sugar in barley grains, only long starch molecules. These must first be broken down into smaller sugar molecules, some of which will ferment and some that will add to the flavor in other ways, like overt or subtle sweetness. To accomplish this, several other steps are necessary. First, the barley must be malted. The grains are moistened and warmed to start the germination process. This creates enzymes that patiently wait in the grain until they are called upon to break starch molecules down into sugar molecules later in the process. Next, the barley grains are cracked open to allow water in, then soaked in water at specific temperatures for specific periods of time. This activates the enzymes, which cut and chop the starch chains into sugar molecules. Creating sugar molecules from starch molecules is known as "saccharification." The steeping time and temperatures of this malt-and-water mash determine just how the starch molecules will break down into fermentable sugar that will be available as food for the yeast, and nonfermentable sugar that will otherwise bolster the flavor. Only after these sugars are created is yeast added. Fermentation can then proceed.

Saké is also made from a grain: rice. However, the enzymes that break down the starch molecules into fermentable sugars in saké making must come from outside the rice grains, which already have been milled to remove the outer portions, and therefore cannot be malted.

These enzymes are provided by a mold called *kōji-kin*, or *Aspergillus oryzae,* that is deliberately cultivated onto steamed rice. This provides the enzymes that will perform the required saccharification, just as malting does in beer production.

Steamed rice onto which this kōji-kin has been propagated is mixed with straight steamed rice, water, and yeast in the same tank. The key point here is that saccharification and fermentation by the yeast take place at the same time in the same tank. In this, saké is unique in the world of alcoholic beverages. This process is known as *heikō fukuhakkōshiki*, or "multiple parallel fermentation."

The overview above is greatly simplified because the process is impossibly complex. It is very difficult to convey in words what saké-brewing craftsmen spend a lifetime learning. So much is done by experience and intuition that simply explaining the process does not do justice to the craft.

But we must try. A fairly detailed description of the process follows, where we'll jump right into an explanation of each step.

Keep in mind that each one of these steps is intimately related to the others. Each step affects everything down the line to a great degree, and in a sense, each and every step is the most important step.

Rice Polishing (*Seimai*)

All rice is, when harvested, brown rice. Even when the outer husk is removed, the kernel itself is of a brownish color. This outer part of the grain must be milled away before the rice is usable for brewing saké.

Good saké rice differs from rice eaten at meals in many ways. An important difference is the concentration of starches in the center of the grain of proper saké rice. Surrounding that starchy center are fats, proteins, and minerals that are generally detrimental to the saké-brewing process. For this reason, the rice is milled to remove this outer portion, effectively removing the undesirables from the equation, while leaving the starches neatly behind.

Over the course of history, various methods have been used to mill, or "polish" rice for saké brewing. Originally, rice was polished using a mortar-and-pestle friction method in which dry brown rice in a small tub was mixed with a special stick until the outer part of the grain was sufficiently removed. Hardly the most efficient of methods, this soon yielded to various types of machines, such as waterwheel mills powered by rivers, as well as a machine used to remove the skin from coffee beans. Modern saké-polishing machines, known as *seimaiki*, have evolved into slick (if expensive) computer-controlled machines that will polish the desired percentage away in the specified amount of time.

This is one of the few steps of the saké-brewing process in which it can be said that modern technology is vastly superior to traditional methods. In fact, it was with the development of a vertical rice-polishing machine in 1933 that saké quality began to vastly improve.

These machines work by allowing the rice to fall down between two spinning grinding stones, then be taken back to the top by a conveyor belt. This continues for hours until the desired amount has been gently polished away. As the rice moves through the machine, the powdered part that is ground off is continuously vacuumed away. The weight of the rice that remains in the vessel is measured and compared to the original weight before the process began. In this way, the degree of polishing can be monitored closely.

This powder, by the way, is called *nuka*, and is used in livestock feed and many foods, among them Japanese-style pickles, traditional Japanese crackers and confectionaries, and also distilled for use in low-budget alcoholic beverages.

For table rice, about 10 percent has been ground away, leaving the white rice with which we are familiar. Saké rice is polished so that, generally, somewhere between 80 percent (for very cheap saké) and 35 percent (for very expensive saké) of the grain remains. This "percent of the remaining grain size" is known as the *seimaibuai* (pronounced "say-my-boo-eye"). This is an important term to remember (see the more detailed explanation later).

[handwritten margin note: From 20% to 65% is removed.]

This polishing process is not as simple a step as it might seem. It must be done gently for several reasons. As the rice grains are polished, the friction between them naturally generates heat. This heat affects the ability of the rice to absorb water, which will affect each subsequent step. Another concern is maintaining the physical structure of the rice grains. Broken or cracked grains do not ferment as well as unbroken grains. Therefore the integral shape of the rice should be maintained as long as possible throughout fermentation.

Washing and Soaking (*Senmai* and *Shinseki*)

After the rice has been polished to the designated degree, it is washed (*senmai*) to remove the nuka, the talc-like powder still clinging to it from the polishing process. It is then soaked in water (*shinseki*) to prepare it for the steaming process.

This deceivingly simple step is a crucial one. The water content of the rice before steaming significantly affects the condition of the resulting steamed rice. This in turn affects the condition of the *kōji* (steamed white rice onto which a mold, called kōji-kin, has been cultivated), and also affects how the rice added directly to the fermenting mash (i.e., not inoculated with kōji mold) will dissolve during fermentation. Depending on the quality of the saké being produced, this step is often performed with great care and precision.

Rice that has not been highly polished is destined for use in low-end saké. It is often dumped in a vat and left to sit overnight as it will not absorb much water anyway. But highly polished rice used in top-grade saké is usually soaked in smaller lots, perhaps 30 kilograms (66 pounds), and the time spent soaking is measured with a stopwatch. Often the craftsman in charge of preparing the rice in this way can sense the water content within 1 or 2 percent, and will make subtle adjustments as necessary.

Steaming the Rice (*Mushimai* or *Jōmai*)

Steaming the rice is yet another crucial step in saké making, for which equipment and technology have changed and improved. But there are still definite limits to how much automation can be used in this very important step without sacrificing quality in the final product.

The condition of the rice after it has been steamed — how firm or mushy it is, for example — affects every brewing step on down the line. Naturally, how well the rice can be steamed has already been influenced by how well it was polished, washed, and soaked in preparation. But the steaming process itself is still vital.

The vat in which rice is steamed in the large quantities needed for saké production is called a *koshiki*. Originally, koshiki were made of wood, and steam was sent up from a hole in the bottom to steam the rice inside. Note that the rice is not mixed with water, but instead is blasted with steam directly. The steam is distributed so that it flows through the rice as evenly as possible. Modern koshiki come in various shapes and sizes, and are usually made of steel.

Large *kura* (saké breweries) often use a machine that continuously steams the rice as it moves down a conveyor belt. This eliminates the need for brewers to steam numerous small batches on a daily basis. There are also other variations, like rice liquefiers, although these are rarely used in the production of premium saké.

After the rice has been steamed, it is cooled by spreading it out on large pieces of cloth in the cool kura air, or by running it through a machine that breaks up the clumps and cools it down quickly.

Kōji Production (*Seikiku*, or *Kōji-zukuri*)

Kōji production is the heart of the saké-brewing process. There is an old saying in the saké world that aptly describes the importance of kōji making: "Ichi: kōji, ni: moto, san: zukuri." First the kōji, second, the moto, or yeast starter, third, fermentation. This remarkably delicate and complex process takes years to master.

Just what is kōji? Kōji is steamed white rice onto which a mold, called kōji-kin (kōji-mold, simply enough), has been cultivated. Known as *Aspergillus oryzae* in the scientific world, this mold works its way into the rice grains, releasing enzymes as it does so.

A starch molecule is a long chain that cannot be fermented as is; the yeast cells cannot process these long chains and convert them into alcohol and carbon dioxide. They must first be broken down into smaller chains of two or three molecules by the enzymes created by the kōji. These smaller molecules, no longer starches but now various types of sugars, can be processed by yeast cells.

In a given tank of fermenting mash, about 30 percent of the rice has been turned into kōji beforehand, with the rest being regular steamed rice. The enzymes created by this 30 percent will create sugar from both the rice onto which the kōji mold was cultivated as well as the regular steamed rice later added directly to the fermenting mash, known as the *moromi*.

Temperature is extremely important in the production of kōji, and for this reason it is made in a special room within the kura. Known as the *kōji muro*, it is maintained at a higher temperature and humidity than the rest of the kura.

The temperature at which the kōji is cultivated over the forty- to sixty-hour process is crucial. Just what temperatures are maintained and at what stages of the process will determine how vigorously and how thoroughly the kōji will promote saccharification, which in turn determines how sweet, dry, rich, or light a saké will be. The kōji itself gives off heat as it develops, and this must be taken into account while attempting to maintain the desired temperature curve.

Rice designated for kōji duty will be brought to the kōji muro after cooling, and sprinkled with the dark green, extremely fine kōji-kin spores when the temperature is right. After having the mold spores sprinkled onto it, the rice is then mixed and checked to keep temperatures consistent throughout for about two days.

Although machines can create passable kōji using various degrees of automation, and in fact most mass-produced saké is made with machine-made kōji, the best kōji is made by hand. This can call for dividing 200 kilograms (440 pounds) or so of rice into small boxes or trays, and mixing and rearranging these as often as every two hours, day and night. *Ginjō* (super premium saké) brewing season can be tough on the *kurabito* (brewery workers), to say the least.

The way that the mold propagates, known as the *haze*, is important. It can work its way around the grains, or work its way toward the center. Which is better depends on the grade of saké and intended flavor profile, as well as things like the quality of the water and the yeast.

Every kura has its own special techniques and methods of producing kōji. The process has been studied, both scientifically and empirically, in great depth for hundreds of years. Details and fine points to kōji production are specific to each type and style of saké, and methods change based on the desired final product.

If things go poorly at this stage, the smell of kōji may be evident in the finished product. It is a faint, dark, and slightly moldy smell that hovers in the background of the flavor and fragrance.

The Yeast Starter (*Moto* or *Shubo*)

In order to give the yeast cells a chance of survival against the countless bacteria that would otherwise overpower them and send the fermenting tank awry, a small tank with an extremely high concentration of yeast cells is prepared. For this, kōji, regular steamed rice, and water are mixed in a small vat, and to this is added a culture of pure yeast cells. Usually a small amount of lactic acid, to protect the fledgling yeast cells from ill-intentioned bacteria floating in the air, is added as well. Over a two- to three-week period, the kōji breaks down the starches to provide food for the yeast cells, which multiply rapidly until the mixture is ready to have increasingly larger amounts of rice, kōji, and water added to it. At this point, there are as many as five million yeast cells per teaspoon (1 cc) of liquid *moto*.

Other methods also create the moto, but this describes the gist of the most commonly used process.

Moromi and *Sandan Shikomi*

The moto is then transferred to a larger vat, where rice, kōji, and water are added, typically three times. From this point the mash is known as the moromi. These three additions of rice, water, and kōji — a method known as *sandan shikomi* (three-step brewing) — are done over a four-day period. One addition of rice, water, and kōji is made on the first day, one on the third day, and one on the fourth. The second day on which nothing is added is known as *odori*, literally meaning "dance," and is set aside to allow the yeast to propagate.

In general, the second addition of rice, water, and kōji is about twice as big as the first, and the third is about twice as big as the second. There are, of course, variations on this formula.

After all the rice, water, and kōji have been added, the moromi sits and ferments anywhere from eighteen to thirty-two days. When to stop fermentation is a crucial decision. Allowing fermentation to continue for too long can lead to strange off flavors in the saké.

Because the kōji converts the starches gradually, the yeast is not inhibited by the presence of too much sugar, and can continue to produce alcohol and carbon dioxide. This gives saké an alcohol content of up to 20 percent, although fermenting temperatures and yeast types have a lot to do with this. No other fermented beverage in the world has a higher naturally occurring alcohol content.

Pressing (*Jōsō*)

At this point, the moromi is ready to be pressed through a mesh that will separate the newly born saké from the solid remains of the fermented rice, which are known as *kasu*. There are several ways of doing this. The traditional way, still used quite often today, is to put the moromi into meter-long (39-inch-long) cotton bags and lay these in a large box called a *fune*, which is usually made of wood. The lid is then cranked down from the top into the box, pressing the saké out through a hole in the bottom, and leaving the kasu behind in the bags.

When saké is pressed using a fune, the pressing is usually divided into three subbatches. The first one-third of saké taken is known as the *arabashiri* ("rough runoff" is a loose but appropriate translation), and is the saké that runs off before any pressure has been applied to the top of the cotton bags holding the moromi. Next, the lid is cranked down into the box, slowly and gradually, and what comes out over several hours is known as the *nakadare*, or *nakagumi*, and is generally the most prized portion. Finally, the cotton bags are removed and rearranged inside the box so as to squeeze out a bit more, and again the lid is cranked down. What comes out after this final crank-down is known as the *seme*.

Most saké these days, however, is pressed using a large machine that resembles an accordion. Technically known as an *assakuki*, it is more often referred to as a *Yabuta*, the company that makes most of the units in use. The moromi is pumped directly in, and rubber balloonlike bags inflate to squeeze the saké out through dozens of mesh panels, leaving the kasu neatly behind. The labor efficiency of this kind of machine is vastly superior to that of the old fune, but the fune does lead to arguably (if subtly) better saké, in the opinion of most.

Another method of pressing is known as *shizuku*, or "drip." The cotton bags are filled with the moromi and then suspended, allowing the saké to drip out with no pressure at all applied to the moromi in the bags. This method is also known as *kubi-tsuri* or *fukuro-tsuri*, and generally leads to even more elegant and complex saké. But obviously much more labor and much lower yields are the price to be paid for this subtle added quality.

Filtering (*Roka*)

After sitting for about ten days to allow residual chemical reactions to finish and sediments to settle, the saké is filtered (*roka*). This is a curious process in which powdered carbon is added first to the saké, and the resulting black liquid is run through a filter. Unwanted flavor elements can be filtered out, and saké's natural amber color can be removed, leaving a transparent saké that some connoisseurs prefer. Care must be taken, however, since overly aggressive filtering can strip away too much and rob a saké of its distinctiveness.

In fact, many, many brewers these days do not filter their saké, in particular the higher grades. Saké spared this carbon filtration is often much more appealing and interesting. It can be delightfully less refined, but when great water, rice, and brewing skill come together, refined, elegant saké can be the result even without this step.

Pasteurization (*Hi-ire*)

Most saké is pasteurized at this point in the process. This is accomplished by momentarily heating the saké to about 65 degrees Celsius (150 degrees Fahrenheit), usually by passing it through a coiled metal pipe that sits in a vat of heated water. Alternatively bottled saké can be immersed in hot water for a given amount of time, or the saké heated as it is pumped into

The
SAKÉ-MAKING PROCESS

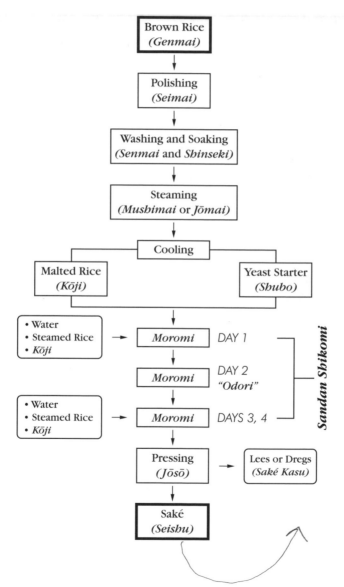

MAKING DIFFERENT TYPES
of SAKÉ

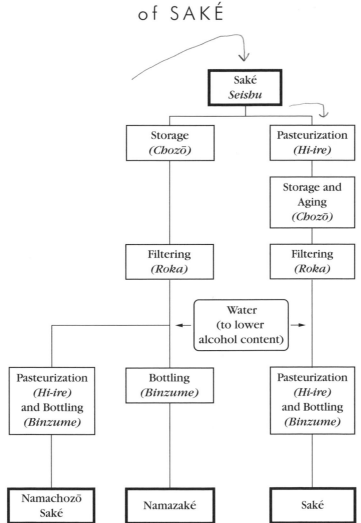

bottles on a bottling line. Regardless of the method, pasteurization is called *hi-ire*.

Long ago, all saké was unpasteurized. In those days of old, one problem recurred: if saké was not kept cold, it usually became cloudy, and the flavor and fragrance turned strange. Somehow the brewers of that era came up with the idea of briefly heating the saké, and found that saké thusly treated remained unspoiled even if not refrigerated.

Without realizing it, and long before Louis Pasteur could have told them, brewers were deactivating enzymes and killing riffraff bacteria, preventing them from adversely affecting the saké. If unpasteurized saké (*namazaké*) is not kept cold, it can suffer a condition known as *hi-ochi*, in which it becomes cloudy, yeasty, and cloying.

Usually, this process is done twice, once before storage, and once again before shipping. Procedures, however, do vary a bit from kura to kura.

At this time, water is usually added to bring the naturally occurring alcohol level of about 20 percent down to about 16 percent.

◆ ◆ ◆

The description above outlines the basic steps of the saké-brewing process. Details on any one of these steps and its many variations could easily fill a book or more. Naturally, condensing the process to just a few pages does not do justice to the craft, but it is an adequate foundation for informed saké tasting.

CHAPTER TWO

TYPES OF SAKÉ, NOMENCLATURE, AND TERMINOLOGY

A newcomer to the world of saké immediately runs into a large number of terms that can indeed be a roadblock to enjoying the beverage. Getting beyond this barrier is not as daunting as it might seem though, and just a little exposure to both the terms themselves and the saké indicative of them will go a long way toward increasing knowledge and deepening enjoyment of saké.

There are a handful of terms defining style and grade that have been agreed upon by the Japan Saké Brewers' Association, and a spattering of other terms that are used a bit more loosely. Some are important; others are less so. Most of these terms refer to how the rice is processed, or to one of several methods by which the saké is made.

Although the prefecture in which a saké was brewed is printed on the label, it is usually relegated to small type in the corner. This is not to imply that no one pays attention to what part of the country a saké was made in, or from where the *tōji* (brew master) hails. On the contrary, these are actually very important details to many saké fans.

But in Japan, saké rice from one region can — and very often is — transported to another part of the country for brewing as there are no restrictions preventing it. In fact, the rice used in brewing is rarely grown by the kura doing the brewing. This gives any kura anywhere access to the best saké rice types in the country — in theory anyway. (In reality it is a bit more difficult than that, but not for legal reasons.)

The Obsolete Ranking System

Until the early 1990s, all saké was officially ranked by the government as "special class" (*Tokkyū*), "first class" (*Ikkyū*), or "second class" (*Nikyū*). Although this system, known as the *kyūbetsu seido,* was a fairly reliable indication of what you were buying, its drawbacks eventually led to its demise, with it finally being totally phased out in 1992.

Under this system, saké designated as Tokkyū or Ikkyū was awarded these distinctions after being successfully submitted for evaluation. If the quality was deemed high enough by the government tasters, the brewer could label the saké special class or first class. Naturally, the government placed a hefty tax on the higher grades. All saké not meeting the standards of one of these top two classes was labeled Nikyū by default.

Many brewers, however, did not bother to submit their saké for classification, which resulted in some very fine saké being humbly labeled Nikyū, right along with bottom-shelf rotgut. Although you could rarely go wrong with a Tokkyū saké, if you knew what to look for, something even better might be available for less.

For reasons such as these, among others, the system ceased to be useful for either consumers or the tax office, and was eliminated. This has only slightly simplified things, and the best way to determine quality is still simply tasting and sniffing to determine your own preferences.

HELPFUL SAKÉ TERMS

In the end, the fragrance and flavor of a saké — and whether or not it appeals to you — is all you really need to know. But a myriad of terms used to classify saké still exists. Knowing what defines the various grades, and what the terms mean, can be useful in identifying what you might like.

Nihonshu

The word "saké" itself in Japanese can refer to all alcoholic beverages in general. When it is inherently understood that the topic is saké as we know it outside of Japan — and not beer, wine, or whiskey — then the word saké alone will suffice. But if it is necessary to differentiate, the word *nihonshu* is used.

Nihonshu simply means "the saké of Japan," and was adopted by the industry in the 1970s. It seems to be more commonly used in Japan than elsewhere, as there is never any confusion outside of Japan as to what the word "saké" means.

Seishu

Seishu is a term that appears on every single bottle of saké. It is, in short, legalese for saké. The literal meaning is "refined saké," which is why that English phrase appears on many bottles of saké from long ago. This term is not commonly used outside of legal or tax-related writings about saké.

Futsūshu

Futsūshu means "ordinary saké," and refers to average, run-of-the-mill, "table saké." This type of saké makes up more than 75 percent of all saké on the market, and while much of this is cheap, bland, and hangover inducing, there are many perfectly drinkable — if simple and straightforward — futsūshu saké available.

Even within the range of futsūshu a few other classes exist. Some of these allow acids and sugars to be used for flavor adjusting, some do not. Futsūshu is typically the kind of saké found served very hot in Japanese restaurants.

THE GENERAL GROUPING OF *TOKUTEI MEISHŌSHU*

All of the following classifications of "premium" saké can be lumped together and referred to as *tokutei meishōshu*. This, then includes junmaishu, honjōzō, tokubetsu junmaishu, tokubetsu honjōzō, and all four kinds of ginjōshu. This term does not appear on labels. It is generally used only in texts or conversations to differentiate premium saké from average saké (futsūshu), described earlier.

Junmaishu

Junmaishu is pure rice saké; nothing is used in its production except rice, water, and kōji-kin, that magical mold that converts the starch in the rice into fermentable sugars. This is similar, at least in spirit, to German beer regulations that allow nothing but malted barley, hops, and water to be used. Saké that is not labeled junmaishu (or have the word *junmai* somewhere on the bottle) will have pure distilled alcohol added in varying amounts, as well as possibly sugar and organic acids, depending on how little one is willing to pay. These increase both yields in brewing and hangovers in consumers.

The designation "junmaishu" further requires that the rice used in brewing be polished, or milled, so that no more than 70 percent of the original size of the grains remains, hopefully ensuring that a certain degree of smoothness will result in the final product. Rice so polished is referred to has having a seimaibuai of 70 percent.

Junmaishu is generally a bit heavier and fuller in flavor than other types of saké, and often the acidity is a bit higher. More solidly built, assertive saké like typical junmaishu is easier to match with meals than much lighter saké. It is not necessarily, however, what everyone prefers.

Honjōzō

Honjōzō, also known as *honjōzukuri*, is saké to which a very small amount of pure distilled alcohol has been added to the final stage of the moromi, just before it is pressed to separate the saké from the lees (nonfermentable rice solids remaining in the saké). The amount of added alcohol is strictly limited to about 120 liters (32 gallons) for every metric ton (2,200 pounds) of rice used in brewing. This pure, distilled alcohol usually comes from distillers specializing in its production.

Adding a *small* amount of alcohol to premium saké like this is not just a matter of increasing yields; there are sound technical reasons for doing it. First of all, it can lighten the flavor, making a saké a bit more drinkable, in the opinion of many. This is one reason that honjōzō is often a good choice for warming.

Also, adding a bit of alcohol at that precise stage tends to pull out more fragrant and flavorful components from the moromi when pressing, as many of them are soluble in alcohol.

Note that honjōzō (and any other grade of saké with alcohol added to it, for that matter) is not really a fortified beverage, as enough water is added later to bring the alcohol content down to the same levels as most saké.

Like junmaishu, a further requirement for honjōzō is a seimaibuai of 70 percent, which means that the rice used in brewing has been polished so that no more than 70 percent of the original size of the grains remains. This removes the fats and proteins that would otherwise potentially contribute to off flavors.

Some people in the industry, and in the ranks of discerning consumers, espouse the concept that true saké connoisseurs will drink nothing but junmaishu. Their reasoning is that only junmaishu is real saké, and adding alcohol is but an aberration of the craft.

Originally all saké was junmaishu. However, for hundreds of years, distilled alcohol (in the form of another distilled beverage called *shōchū*) was on occasion added to tanks of saké if and when it was needed to bolster the saké or protect it from going bad. What constitutes real saké historically, then, is a matter of whom you ask.

While it is true that in cheap saké alcohol is indeed added solely to increase yields, in premium saké (like honjōzō and higher grades) much smaller amounts of alcohol are added with very definite objectives. In the end, it is just another way of doing things, just one more method a kura has at its disposal.

Ginjōshu

Ginjōshu, more than just a separate classification, is a separate world. Essentially a ginjōshu-designated saké is one for which the rice used in brewing has a seimaibuai of at least 60 percent, which again means that no more than 60 percent of the original size of the grains remains after milling. This, however, is simply the minimum requirement for a saké to have the word ginjōshu on the label. Much more goes into the brewing of most ginjōshu.

Within the classification of ginjōshu there is the subclass *daiginjōshu*. For daiginjōshu, the seimaibuai is a minimum of 50 percent, and often can be as much as 35 percent. This indicates that at least half of the raw materials have been ground away before brewing even begins. There is, of course, much more involved in creating a great daiginjōshu than simply the milling of the rice, but as far as terminology and labeling requirements are concerned, the seimaibuai requirement is what must be met.

Some saké is labeled as *chūginjō*, and this simply refers to a saké that is somewhere between a ginjōshu and a daiginjōshu. There is, however, no strict definition of the seimaibuai for a chūginjō.

The issue of whether or not alcohol has been added applies to this class of saké as well. Ginjōshu and daiginjōshu to which no alcohol has been added during the brewing process are known as *junmai ginjō* and *junmai daiginjō* respectively. If that small amount of alcohol has in fact been added during the final stages of brewing, the word junmai will not appear on the label, and such saké will be called simply ginjōshu or daiginjōshu.

Please note that such saké is generally *not* referred to as *honjōzō ginjō*, or *honjōzō daiginjō* as one might be tempted to think, but rather just ginjō and daiginjō, even though the volume limitations on the added alcohol are the same as *honjōzōshu*.

Tokubetsu Junmaishu and *Tokubetsu Honjōzō*

Tokubetsu means "special" in Japanese, and what is special about these two types of saké is a bit nebulous. The agreed-upon definition is that these are junmaishu or honjōzō which have something special about them. This might be a higher than usual seimaibuai of 60 percent, or it might be that half or more of the rice used in brewing was specially designated saké rice. It also may be that some special method was used, and if so, this should be indicated on the label. Unfortunately this is not always the case, and sometimes consumers are left wondering what it is that makes a so-labeled saké special. However, in the end, what is important is that tokubetsu honjōzō and tokubetsu junmaishu are a bit higher grade than regular honjōzō and junmaishu.

If such saké can be labeled ginjōshu or junmai ginjōshu by virtue of its 60 percent seimaibuai, then why do brewers not do so? In many cases, the reason is most kura produce a range of saké, one of which may already be designated as their flagship ginjōshu. In order not to interfere with the image and marketing of such a product, such saké might be referred to as the marginally lower grade tokubetsu honjōzō or tokubetsu junmaishu.

OTHER SAKÉ TERMS

Here are a handful of other terms that, while less common and less stringently defined, you might see from time to time.

Namazaké and *Namachozō*

Namazaké is unpasteurized saké. The flavor of namazaké is somewhat fresher and livelier than its pasteurized counterpart. This can be overpowering so that all you taste is the *nama*-ness (so to speak) of the saké, but it can also be a barely discernible difference. How overpowering this attribute is varies from saké to saké, depending a great deal on how the saké was processed and stored after having been brewed. Namazaké must be kept refrigerated, or the chances of the flavor and clarity being adversely affected by bacterial and enzymatic activity remain high. In other words, it can spoil. Namazaké gone bad is cloudy, with grossly exaggerated sweet, tart, and yeasty flavors and smells.

Most saké is actually pasteurized twice: once just after brewing and before it is stored for maturation, and then once again at bottling time, before shipping. A variation called *namachozō* is saké that was stored without being pasteurized, then pasteurized only one time, at bottling. This saké finds a middle ground between namazaké and twice-pasteurized saké. The characteristic namazaké freshness and zing are less noticeable, although namachozō does have more of these qualities than fully pasteurized saké. Although *namachozō* is less delicate than *namazaké*, it too should be refrigerated.

Taruzake

Taruzake is saké that has been stored or aged for some time in a cedar cask called a *taru*, and therefore takes on a relatively strong flavor imparted by the wood. This is not an unpleasant flavor, and definitely has its time and place, but it can be overpowering as well. Just keep in mind that the woody touches usually will be much more noticeable than any subtle aspects.

Before the age of bottling, all saké was stored in wooden taru, and as such, taruzake is a bit of a throwback to the past.

Nigorizaké

When the moromi is ready to be pressed into saké, the white rice solids that did not ferment, the lees of the process, are separated from the clear or slightly amber fresh nihonshu. *Nigorizaké* is saké in which some of this white stuff — called *saké kasu* — is left in the saké by filtering with a very coarse mesh or large-holed filter. (Alternatively, some of it can actually be added back to the clear saké.) Nigorizaké can be found in all consistencies, from only slightly murky, to chunky enough to eat with a fork. While nigorizaké may lack the subtle aspects of a pristine ginjōshu, it has its own charms and legions of fans. The flavors of nigorizaké flavors can be all over the map: some are sweet, many are quite tart. But nigorizaké is fun, and can have a myriad of hidden flavors as well.

Genshu

Before bottling and shipping, pure water is usually added to saké to adjust the alcohol content from the naturally occurring 20 percent or so down to about 16 percent. *Genshu* is saké to which water has not been added.

An alcohol content of about 20 percent is often (but not always) a bit too strong to sense the finer flavors and nuances of a saké; they tend to get a bit bludgeoned. For this reason, some people serve genshu on the rocks, as this can take the bite out of it and also water it down a bit. Some varieties of saké have the requisite body and soul to actually be enhanced by a higher alcohol content, which gives them a greater impact.

Another interesting point to keep in mind is that not all genshu is 20 percent alcohol. Some types of genshu saké are 15 to 16 percent alcohol, or even lower. This is accomplished through a variety of methods, including fermenting at lower temperatures, using special types of yeast that cease functioning at lower alcohol levels, or simply stopping the fermentation process before the alcohol content rises too high.

Yamahai-Shikomi and *Kimoto*

Yamahai-shikomi saké is hardly mainstream, but its uniqueness of flavor makes it a very interesting style of saké, and one worth knowing about. *Kimoto* saké is technically related to yamahai, and historically its predecessor. Yamahai-shikomi and kimoto saké also are similar in typical flavor profiles.

The differences between these two types and other saké relates to the moto (the yeast starter) which is the small vat of rice, water, and kōji to which yeast is added and in which it is propagated. Together they become the seed of a batch of saké.

Originally it was thought that the rice and kōji had to be pureed for them to work properly together and convert the starches to sugars. To achieve this, the kurabito (brewery workers) would ram oar-like poles into the mixture for hours on end — exhausting work to say the least. This pole ramming is known as *yama-oroshi*. Moto made in this way was (and still is) called kimoto. Originally all moto was kimoto; it was the only way they knew how to make it.

Then, in 1909, scientists at the National Institute of Brewing Research discovered all that hard work simply wasn't necessary; if left alone, the enzymes in the kōji would eventually dissolve all the rice. The only catch was that you had to add a bit more water and keep the temperature a bit warmer, a comparatively painless process.

When it became known then that the rough part (yama-oroshi) could be eliminated (*hai-shi*), *yama-oroshi hai-shi*, shortened to *yamahai*, was born. (*Shikomi,* as in yamahai-shikomi, simply means "to make a batch.")

Both kimoto and yamahai moto take about a month to develop. This can be a nerve-wracking time because stray bacteria and wild yeast cells hell-bent on destruction can ruin a whole batch. Sanitation is paramount, and pains must be taken to keep the developing moto covered and protected.

Next, in 1911 it was discovered that by adding a bit of lactic acid to the moto at the beginning, the whole process could be accomplished in about half the time. Lactic acid is a product of the yeast life cycle, and when present in sufficient amounts, it prevents wild yeasts and unwanted bacteria from proliferating and adversely affecting the flavor. Lactic acid develops naturally in kimoto and yamahai saké, albeit a bit more slowly.

Adding lactic acid at the beginning speeds the process up, allowing the moto to be ready for use in about two weeks. It also protects it from the start, putting everyone at ease. This alter ego of yamahai/kimoto is known as *sokujō*-moto, or "fast-developing" moto.

Although there are minor variants, kimoto/yamahai and sokujō are the two basic types of moto. Due to a characteristic resistance to new-fangled technology, it took about ten years for sokujō-moto to gain acceptance on an industry-wide basis. Now, however, almost all saké is made this faster way.

Flavor-wise, what are the differences? Yamahai and *kimoto* are similar and have a higher sweetness and acidity, with richer, deeper, significantly more pronounced flavors. Sokujō-moto (i.e., most saké on the market) is comparatively milder and cleaner in flavor. However, there are oodles of overlap; yamahai/kimoto saké can be clean and refined, and sokujō-moto saké can be wild and gamy. So in the end, extreme cases notwithstanding, it's not a whole lot to get worked up about.

Many kura, but not all, make at least some yamahai or kimoto saké. Because such moto must be kept isolated from the rest of the moto due to the number of wild yeast involved, it often is not worth the time for many saké brewers. It also calls for harder water, and most importantly, it may not be the style of saké the kura is interested in producing.

So, the long and short of it all is this: for yamahai and kimoto saké, the yeast starter was created in a slow and laborious way that allowed more wild yeasts and bacteria to become a part of the brew. This usually leads to a richer, tangier flavor.

Shiboritate

Shiboritate means just pressed. Saké with the word "shiboritate" on the label is saké that has been freshly pressed away from the kasu. Usually it is fresh and brash and youthful. However, keep in mind that this term alone indicates nothing about the grade of the saké, or whether or not it has been pasteurized.

Muroka

Muroka refers to saké that has not been charcoal filtered. Muroka should not be confused with nigorizaké. *Nigori* is saké that is "unfiltered" in that much of the rice solids in the moromi were allowed to remain; muroka refers to clear saké that has not been fine-filtered with active charcoal before storage and/or shipping. Saké like this can be a bit fuller and perhaps rougher, but if the water and brewing process were good enough, charcoal filtering might not be necessary anyway.

Koshu

Koshu is aged saké. This term does not have an overly strict definition, and will vary from kura to kura, although it generally refers to saké aged at least three years. Run-of-the-mill saké does not age well, becoming cloying and unbalanced. But premium saké can age into an earthy, balanced, and settled flavor and fragrance that can be very pleasant. Often there are sherry tones and woodiness, and an overall stronger flavor profile. Although quite a bit depends on just how the saké was aged (in a tank or in the bottle, at what temperature, and for how long), most aged saké takes on a much darker color as well.

Lately, deliberately aged saké has come to be referred to as *chōki jukuseishu*, a euphemism that simply means "long-term matured saké." Although such saké has its fans, it constitutes but a very, very small share of the market. It is still safe to say that most saké should be consumed young and fresh, within a year of bottling at most.

Jizaké

Perhaps the vaguest of the vague, the term *jizaké* is tossed around quite a bit. In its strictest definition, jizaké means local saké, or saké from the countryside, inferring small brewers. It implies that the saké is made from rice grown in its region and with local water, and until a few decades ago most such saké was not available outside of that region. Now distribution infra-structures have changed so that any saké is for the most part available anywhere in Japan.

Another original nuance of the term jizaké was simply saké that was not brewed by the large, national brand breweries. While such saké has not always maintained the year-to-year stability and consistency of large breweries, a certain amount of romanticism, distinction, and flair remains aligned with the term jizaké.

Sanzōshu

This term is a subclass (in several senses of the word) of futsūshu, and is decidedly unflattering. You will not find this term printed on any label!

During the Second World War, rice was understandably scarce. Many saké brewers were forced by the government to combine operations with other brewers, or to cease brewing altogether. Those that continued were forced by law to use new methods that used much less rice, and added pure distilled grain alcohol to increase the yields. Eventually they got to the point where so much alcohol was added that the amount of saké brewed from a given amount of rice was tripled. This was known as *sanbai zōjōshu*, and shortened to *sanzōshu*.

Today sanzōshu refers to such bottom-shelf saké, with its excessive amount of added sugars, acids, and alcohol.

◆ ◆ ◆

The terms defined in this chapter are by no means exhaustive, but the most commonly met terms have been explained. Please do not assign an excessive amount of importance to these terms, however, since they are but a guideline. Terminology can give you an idea of what to expect in terms of flavor, but it can also be a distraction. All too often terminology leads to preconceived ideas about how a saké should taste, which is always a drawback when it comes to proper saké tasting. The only real standard for judging is whether or not a saké appeals to you personally.

Kurabito break up clumps of
developing kōji in a *muro*.
(Courtesy of Chōryu Shuzō.)

Mixing the moromi as it ferments
to ensure consistency in the *oke*,
or tank.

CHAPTER THREE

GINJŌSHU: ITS CHARMS, JOYS, AND PRODUCTION

injō saké, or ginjōshu, is in a class of its own. You can't spend more than a few minutes in the world of nihonshu without coming across the term. With its delicate nature and refined flavors and fragrances, it can represent the pinnacle of the brewer's skill.

Until about thirty years ago, ginjōshu was just a novelty brewed in small amounts, usually for contests and demonstrations of technique and skill within the industry. It was considered to be far too labor intensive to ever really be worth making on a large-scale basis. Slowly, however, through the efforts of a few individuals in the late 1960s, more and more breweries began producing ginjōshu in marketable quantities.

Eventually ginjō reached critical mass in the market, connoisseurs became hooked, and what became known as the "ginjō boom" was born. This, combined with improvements in the transportation and distribution infrastructure of Japan, created both the demand and the supply for good ginjōshu all over the country.

However, although ginjō is indeed top-grade saké, it is by no means the only saké worth drinking. Nor does everyone always prefer such saké over seemingly lesser grades of saké, which can be more simple and sturdy by comparison.

Nihonshu is a very old and traditional beverage. And traditions die hard, as do the opinions of those who support such traditions. There is a firmly entrenched idea of how a good saké should taste that is held by many who have been drinking it since long before ginjōshu appeared on the stage. The lighter, fruitier, fragrant, and flowery profile typical of ginjōshu often does not fit this mold well. As ginjōshu inches in the direction of wine, many believe that it begins to stray from its original essence, becoming something altogether different.

But this old image of saké is fading, fading in the light of what saké can be. And saké is evolving into a new world of subtlety and diversity, more enjoyable and interesting than ever before.

Technically how is ginjōshu different? The only actual hard rule, as mentioned in the section on terminology, is that the rice used in brewing is polished until the outer 40 percent or more of the grain has been ground away. This means, then, that not more than the inner 60 percent remains. As explained earlier, this "percentage of remaining rice grain size" is called the seimaibuai, and can be as low as 35 percent, in which case the outer 65 percent was ground away before beginning, and will not be used in the brewing process. Extravagant? Wasteful? Decadent? Perhaps. But perhaps not.

The reason for all this polishing is related to the fact that rice contains all kinds of components, including starches, fats, proteins, minerals, and amino acids. After saccharification, only the starches will ferment, and the other components will contribute to the flavor in other ways, ways that are desirable to a degree, and less so in excess. Too many fats, proteins, and minerals left in the rice will give a saké strange flavors, making it taste rough.

Fortunately, in proper saké rice, the starches are concentrated in the center of the grain; the fats, proteins, and minerals are generally found in the outer portion of the grain. So by milling the rice more and more, it is possible to remove the fermentation-impeding fats, proteins, and minerals, and leave the cleanly fermenting starches behind in the center.

This is why special rice is used for brewing premium saké like ginjōshu. Nature has conveniently split things up quite nicely in good saké rice varieties like Yamada Nishiki and others used specifically for saké brewing. In good saké rice, the white, opaque center comprised of starch is clearly visible in most of the grains.

Much more goes into the creation of ginjōshu than the rice milling stipulations. Ginjōshu production is vastly different in terms of both methodology and required effort. Of course, the basic steps, principles, and ideas are the same. But ginjōshu production can be nerve-racking and downright exhausting. Most of the steps in the ginjōshu brewing process are done by hand, involving a lot of physical activity and relieving the machines of their onerous duties for a spell. Precision is paramount. At times it seems to border on masochistic, as if there are two ways to a particular step; the one which is more difficult, more exhausting, and more uncomfortable for the brewers will inevitably lead to better saké.

Every step of the process is performed a bit differently for *ginjō-zukuri*, or ginjōshu production. It has been meticulously prepared in a special way, being highly polished, and is therefore more vulnerable and sensitive to various negative influences.

Let's look first at the polishing step. Rice for ginjōshu is polished much more slowly — often as much as three times as long as for other saké — for several reasons. As described earlier, when rice is polished, the friction generates heat, which can make the rice hard and brittle. This in turn will adversely affect its ability to absorb water and maintain proper moisture levels, as well as increase the tendency for the rice to crack and break. Since better fermentation results when the grains maintain their shape, the more slowly and delicately this process is performed, the finer will be the resulting saké.

As has been pointed out, rice must be milled so that no more than 60 percent of the original size of the grain remains for ginjōshu, and 50 percent for daiginjōshu. But these numbers are minimums, and often daiginjōshu is made with much more highly polished rice. However, this does not imply that the more is milled away, the better the saké. Milling too much away can lead to saké devoid of character and flavor. Finding that balance is one more challenge involved in brewing great saké.

Next is the soaking step, known as shinseki. The water content of the rice when it goes into the steaming vat is crucial, as the condition of the steamed rice will dictate how well the kōji develops, as well as how well fermentation overall proceeds. For ginjōshu, the amount of time the rice spends submerged in water is often measured to the second with a stopwatch. How long the rice sits submerged in water will vary according to the rice, the seimaibuai, the step of the process to which the rice is going, and a million other factors.

The making of kōji is where things get really intense in ginjōshu production. For regular saké, the kōji is made in fairly large batches, and is sometimes done by machine. Not so with the kōji used for ginjōshu. In order to control the temperature as precisely and evenly as possible, a single batch of kōji might be prepared using dozens of *kōjibuta*, small wooden trays (about the size of a writing tablet, and about two inches deep) designed for this purpose. A single batch of kōji — anywhere from 100 to 300 kilograms (220 to 660 pounds) — will be split up among these trays for part of the time spent in the kōji-making room, with the trays stacked high, and stacks placed close together.

Then the contents of each tray will be mixed and shaken according to a particular tried-and-true physical algorithm every few hours. The trays will also be repositioned within the stacks at this time. The whole point is to keep the temperature and moisture distribution controlled and evenly distributed throughout the batch, allowing each grain of rice to have the kōji mold propagate around and into it in the same way. This moving and shaking is done every two hours until the kōji is ready. The entire process takes from thirty-six to fifty hours, depending on a whole host of factors.

The rice used in each of these steps is handled with care, to keep the grains from being crushed or smashed. In lower grade saké, large air hoses are often used to shoot the rice from where it is cooled into the appropriate tank, but in ginjō production, such methods are forsaken for older ways, like wrapping up the steamed rice in a large swath of cloth and hand-carrying it to its destination, thus ensuring the rice will not be crushed along the way.

Fermentation is greatly dependent on temperature. Different types of yeast function best in different temperature ranges. In general, when saké fermentation proceeds at lower temperatures, the yeast does its job more slowly, allowing more control over the process, and leading to more flavorful and fragrant saké. This is why ginjōshu is produced in the coldest part of the winter. Of course, this cold is just one more burden the brewers must bear during ginjōshu season.

The moromi sits and ferments for as long as thirty-six days, almost twice the time allotted to that of regular saké. The yeast types used in brewing ginjōshu are also special, being particularly suited to these temperatures and longer fermentation periods. Ginjōshu yeast will also contribute to the development of the ester-laden, fruity *ginjōka*, or ginjōshu fragrance.

Extra care is also taken in the other steps, including the steps after fermentation proper, such as pressing the new saké from the lees, charcoal (or other) fine filtering (if it is done at all), and storage of ginjōshu.

Often ginjōshu is found in smaller bottles — generally 720 milliliters — called *yongō* bottles. One reason for this is that like wine, saké is sensitive to oxidation, and ginjōshu even more so than average saké, with its lively fragrances and flavors. Consumers are likely to finish a smaller amount more quickly, before such a drop in quality can be noted. Another reason is simple economics: smaller bottles are a bit more affordable.

Ginjōshu at its best does indeed represent the pinnacle of the saké world, and the zenith of the brewers' skill. But this does not mean it is the only saké worth drinking. Not everything with the word ginjōshu on the label is sterling, and there is plenty of saké of slightly lower grade that is extremely enjoyable to drink.

But overall, all of this excruciatingly hard work on the part of the brewers leads to ginjōshu that is more delicate, layered, complex, sophisticated, and interesting.

CHAPTER FOUR

SAKÉ PARAMETERS AND WHAT THEY REALLY MEAN

*T*here is precious little information listed on saké labels that might suggest what the saké inside might be like. Even terms like honjōzō, junmai, ginjō and daiginjō do not give away too much information, as each of these grades has a plethora of potential flavor profiles associated with it.

But a few parameters appear with increasing regularity on saké labels, and premium saké in particular, that can give clues about the probable flavor profile. These include the seimaibuai (by far the most common), *nihonshu-do* (also unofficially known as the "Saké Meter Value" in the U.S., and sometimes abbreviated as "SMV"), acidity, amino acid content, and type of yeast. Occasionally the guild of the tōji (head brewer) is also listed.

When listed on the label, knowing the meaning behind these numbers can aid in assessing whether the flavor and fragrance of a saké suits your preferences and the occasion.

Opinion is somewhat divided about how relevant this type of information actually is. None of these parameters exist in a vacuum, and no single one can tell you too much about how a saké will taste. The permutations are countless, especially when combined with other factors such as water, regional style, and the capricious whims of the brewer.

A growing number of saké experts never even pay attention to these numbers, shunning or even disdaining them in favor of a trained and experienced palate.

Naturally, whether or not a saké is appealing to you is the most important aspect in determining quality. The best way to determine your saké likes and dislikes, as well as how to match saké with food, is simply to taste a wide range of saké. In the end, these parameters can at best give only a vague indication of what to expect, a guideline perhaps.

But these vital statistics are important for another reason: they keep us a bit closer to the brewing process, enabling more intelligent assessments based on the added information. Knowing what they mean creates a set of expectations that we can use as a point of departure in allowing us to understand more fully what affects the final flavor and fragrance of a saké. In the end, access to this kind of brewing data makes us more educated and discerning consumers.

Here is a description of the meaning and significance of each of these parameters. They are commonly found not only on labels, but on store shelves and saké pub menus as well.

Seimaibuai

As described in several other places in this book, the seimaibuai is the degree to which the rice used in brewing has been milled, or "polished" as they say in the industry. This is expressed as a percentage, with the actually number referring to the size of the grains after milling compared to their premilling size.

This means that rice with a 60 percent seimaibuai (the minimum for ginjōshu) has had the outer 40 percent ground away, with the inner 60 percent remaining. Likewise, a 35 percent seimaibuai (not uncommon for top-grade daiginjō) indicates that a full 65 percent of the original grain has been milled away. The ground-away powder, while not wasted, is not used in the brewing process.

This is perhaps one of the most dependable of these parameters, and one from which the most useful generalizations and predictions can be drawn. This is because in general, the more the rice has been milled, the more refined and elegant the final flavor profile.

As elaborated upon earlier, this is related to the fact that in good saké rice, the starches are concentrated in the center of the grains, while fats and proteins — the source of potential off flavors — reside in the outside of the grains. Milling removes more of these, leaving only the clean-fermenting starches behind.

The caveat to all this is that these fats and proteins can also contribute character and flavor to a saké when present in the right measure. A saké brewed with more highly milled rice is not unequivocally better than one brewed with larger rice grains. Indeed, an excessive seimaibuai can lead to saké that is boring in its pristine simplicity. It is all very much a matter of opinion and preference.

Nibonshu-do

This cryptic term indicates whether a saké is dry or sweet. It is sometimes (albeit unofficially) called the Saké Meter Value, abbreviated SMV. Chemically it is the specific gravity of the saké, or the density of the saké compared to that of water. In essence, it is equivalent to the residual sugar measurement in wine.

During the saké-brewing process, kōji mold breaks down the starch molecules in the rice into various types of sugar molecules. The amount and types of sugar that are created is a function of which enzymes resulted from the kōji cultivation, a function of time, temperature, and method. Some of these sugars will later be converted by the yeast into alcohol and carbon dioxide, while other sugars will not.

After the fermentation has run its course, about 20 percent of the undiluted final product is alcohol. There will also be a certain amount of unfermented sugar left over. The combination of lighter alcohol, heavier sugars and other nonfermentable components (like fats and proteins) combine to give a measurable density relative to that of water. This is the nihonshu-do.

The scale used, however, is one that was arbitrarily assigned long, long ago, and bears no resemblance to the scale used for modern residual sugar or specific gravity measurements. The range of nihonshu-do is theoretically open-ended, but in general extends from perhaps –3 to about +12. In short, the higher the number, the drier the saké.

When the scale was first assigned, 0 was considered more or less neutral in flavor. But public tastes and preferences change often, and today a saké with a nihonshu-do of +3 would probably be considered somewhat neutral on the sweet-dry scale. As dry saké is preferred by most consumers, the commonly encountered range of nihonshu-do extends more on the higher (and therefore dry) end of the range than on the lower (and therefore sweet) end.

It is common to see saké with a nihonshu-do of +8 or +10, but saké with a value of –1 or lower is rare by comparison.

Most importantly keep in mind that other parameters (like the acidity, in particular) must be taken into account when attempting to assess the flavor profile of a saké. The reality is that, except in extremes, the nihonshu-do numbers alone do not indicate true sweetness or dryness. Saké, with all of its complexities and transient idiosyncrasies, has become too complex for that, and dozens of other factors play a part.

Acidity (*Sanmi*)

The amount of acid found in a saké very often defines the flavor as a whole. Several kinds of acid develop during the fermentation process, and each imparts slightly different nuances to the flavor.

The general range of acidity in saké is perhaps 0.9 to 2.0. The number used to express the acidity is somewhat arcane, and refers to the amount of the alkaline chemical used in testing needed to neutralize the acidity of a given amount of saké. The range is not huge, but the difference in the actual flavor of a saké on each end of this spectrum is significant.

Many things in the brewing process, such as the choice of yeast, regional considerations, and the style of brewing, affect the resulting acidity in a saké. Also, some types of saké, most notably junmaishu and yamahai-shikomi, often have a slightly higher acidity than other types.

The sense of acidity in saké, however, does not always directly correspond to the actual measurement of acidity. The mineral content of the water, the nihonshu-do, and the alcohol content also affect perceived acidity.

The acidity and the nihonshu-do are commonly listed on labels, and are often considered together to give a vague idea of what kind of overall impression to expect in a saké. A higher acidity often makes a sweeter saké taste more dry, while a lower acidity can make a saké seem heavier on the palate.

In the end, however, consumers need not place undue importance on such analysis. For those who like to study numbers, the numbers are there; for the rest of us, simply tasting and sniffing will suffice. The overall impression of a saké hovers on a level well above mere facts and figures.

Amino Acid (*Amino-san*)

Amino acids result from the breakdown of proteins in the rice by the kōji, and by heat from steaming. Not as commonly listed as the above figures, the amino acid content seems to have a less noticeable connection to flavor. A low amino acid content generally indicates a saké that is lighter or a bit more airy in feel, while higher amino acids give a saké a quality known as *koku ga aru*, a hard-to-translate term indicating a slightly heavy, slightly earthy quality. In more concrete terms, koku ga aru suggests slightly bitter and tart tones hovering in the background.

Amino acid content is also closely related to a flavor quality known as *umami*, a term that is gaining favor in the wine world as well. Umami refers to a subtle richness or tastiness that can be hard to pinpoint but easy to perceive. Too high an amino acid content, however, leads to roughness and off flavors.

INGREDIENTS

Rice

Another detail very often listed on the label is the type of rice that was used in brewing the saké. This can be very suggestive of how the saké will taste, and is one of the most interesting pieces of information that can be provided.

More than most saké-brewing parameters, the rice used provides a certain framework of expectation. This should not be surprising, as rice is to saké what grapes are to wine.

All rice is not created equal. There are, in fact, many different varieties of rice. These differ in many ways, including size, shape, and content. The rice grown in Japan, and used in saké brewing, is short-grain rice, which is shorter in length than long-grain rice grown in other parts of Asia.

Among the many varieties of short-grain rice, some are much more suited for saké brewing, and some are much more suited for cooking. There are many differences between the two. Rice suited to saké brewing, known as *sakamai*, is physically larger than *shokumai*, rice eaten at the table. The grains are perhaps 25 percent larger.

Within the grain as well there are differences. Sakamai has a higher starch content, which might not be surprising as this is what will ferment once converted to sugar. Table rice, on the other hand, has more protein and fat, which presumably makes it a bit tastier.

Not only is the nutritional content different, but the physical distribution of that content differs as well. In table rice, the fats, proteins, and starches are fairly well distributed within each grain. In good sakamai, however, we have already learned that the starches are concentrated in the center of the grain, with the fat, protein, minerals, and other components hovering around the outside.

This centralized starch packet is known as a *shinpaku*, and is visible as a white, opaque region in the center of the grain. This physical construction makes it easy to mill the rice so that the desirable starches remain while the less sought-after proteins and fats can be easily eliminated from the equation through proper milling.

Other differences between sakamai and shokumai can be seen in the plants that yield the grains. Sakamai is more difficult to grow than table rice, for many reasons. Most notably is the physical size of the stalks.

Saké rice stalks are physically taller, often taller than one meter (39 inches). As such they are much harder to cultivate and harvest. The heavier grains make the plant top-heavy, and late in the season they may begin to droop. This makes the plants vulnerable to being blown over and rendered useless before harvest time by a strong typhoon or storm.

Tall stalks like this are hard to harvest, being too tall for a combine or other machine to be effective. This means that such rice must be harvested by hand, which calls for much more manual labor.

Sakamai is also much more sensitive to insecticides and other chemicals, yet calls for excellent earth and thorough irrigation. Yields are not as high as those for table rice, as volume of harvest is not as important as the quality of the rice grains themselves.

As might be imagined, sakamai is much more expensive, often as much as three times the cost of shokumai. Couple this with the liberal milling of the rice before brewing, and it's a wonder premium saké is as cheap as it is.

Within the realm of saké rice, there are of course many varieties. Each of these prefers different climates and earth conditions, and therefore grows best in a particular region. Although Japan is not a large country, it has a wide range of terrains and climates.

Sakamai, formally known as *shuzō-kōtekimai*, is an official designation. The criteria include such things as grain size and the percentage of the harvested grains that have a visible opaque starch packet in the center.

And, each variety of sakamai contributes its own, identifiable characteristics and style to the final saké product. Different sakamai leads to different flavors and aromatic components, especially when used in combination with suitable yeast strains.

Below are some examples of saké rice, the type of saké they yield, and the prefectures in which they grow best.

> *YAMADA NISHIKI.* Grows best in Hyogo,
> Okayama, and Hiroshima Prefectures.
> Currently Yamada Nishiki is recognized by
> many as the overall best sakamai. Fruity,
> lively, and layered flavors and fragrances.

> *GOHYAKUMAN GOKU.* Grows best in
> Niigata, Toyama, and Ishikawa Prefectures.
> Light, dry, and very refined.

> *ŌMACHI.* Grows best in Okayama and
> Hiroshima Prefectures. Full, settled, smooth,
> and almost herbal, with excellent acidity.

MIYAMA NISHIKI. Grows best in Akita, Yamagata, and Nagano Prefectures. Even, chewy flavors with good supporting acidity.

HATTAN AND HATTAN NISHIKI. Grows best in Hiroshima. Slightly subdued and mellow.

KAME NO Ō. Yamagata, Akita, Niigata Prefectures. Full, fat, playful with a lively acidity.

Naturally this list is by no means complete, nor is it static. There are about sixty different types of officially designated saké rice, with an occasional new one added to the list. New varieties are sometimes created by crossbreeding, the result of efforts on the part of saké-brewing or industrial research centers operated by the prefectures or the national government.

In fact almost all saké rice is the result of crossbreeding, with two notable exceptions from the list above being Kame no Ō and Ōmachi. (The story of Kame no Ō is romantic and interesting, and has been retold with some embellishment in the excellent and educational comic book series *Natsuko no Saké*, a must-read for saké fans that can read Japanese.)

Note, too, that only freshly harvested rice is used to brew saké. Rice does not get better with time, and saké brewed with old rice will itself taste as if it has been improperly aged.

Perhaps the most important of the rice types listed above is Yamada Nishiki. It is easily the best saké rice on the planet, at least when measured by its popularity among saké connoisseurs and its success in blind-tasting competitions. While it is by no means the only grain in town, it gives the brewer a lot of flexibility and can lead to widely different but wonderful saké profiles.

Not all saké is brewed with proper sakamai. About 75 percent of all saké brewed, in fact, is simpler, run-of-the-mill saké made using less labor-intensive methods. Most of this is brewed with less expensive table rice. While much of this saké is perfectly and enjoyably drinkable, using proper saké rice generally leads to saké that is more refined and elegant, with more enjoyable flavors and aromas.

Water

Saké in its finished form is about 80 percent pure water. Unlike grapes that yield plenty of liquid juice, steamed rice is fairly firm, and plenty of water is added to create the fermenting mash itself. The amount of water used in all the steps of the brewing process — including washing, soaking, and steaming the rice as well as that used creating the mash — adds up to more than thirty times the rice by weight.

Most of the historically important saké brewing regions came into being due to an abundant supply of good water. In fact, almost without exception, saké breweries exist where they do because long ago a well or spring with fine water was discovered nearby.

The most famous example of good brewing water is that which comes gushing up in the Nada region of the city of Kobe in Hyogo Prefecture after filtering slowly down through a nearby mountain, Mt. Rokko. It is known as *Miyamizu* ("shrine water"), and has an ideal mineral content for saké brewing. Saké brewed with this water did not stay long on the shelves of Edo-period Japan. Chemical analysis was not exactly in its heyday in the 1800s, but the final product told the story and everyone rushed in to set up shop where success had been proven. This has made the Nada region the top brewing region in the country, in terms of volume.

Eventually science caught up to intuition and experience, and it found ways to determine exactly what makes good water for saké brewing, as well as what does not. There are a number of elements whose presence is indispensable, as well as some that are only detrimental.

By far the most detrimental element is iron. Iron will darken the color of saké and adversely affect its taste and fragrance.

This happens because it chemically attaches itself to the center of a normally colorless compound which is itself attached to an amino acid produced while the kōji is being made. Also, as nihonshu ages, the residual sugars react with amino acids present to change the flavor and smell, and the presence of iron hastens this reaction.

Manganese plays a different but equally despicable role. When saké is exposed to light, in particular ultraviolet light, manganese promotes a chemical reaction that will discolor and dull the appearance of a saké. In direct sunlight, this change can be seen in less than three hours.

Although there are others, these two are the main culprits in less-than-optimum saké-brewing water.

Then there are the good guys. In particular, potassium, magnesium, and phosphoric acid are necessary to aid the propagation of the yeast in the shubo (yeast starter), as well as in the proper development of good kōji. If these are not present in sufficient amounts, the yeast cells will not multiply as well or as quickly as they would otherwise, throwing off the timing of the entire fermentation so that it cannot be properly controlled.

Since potassium is water soluble, and can be washed away during the rice washing and soaking process, the brewery workers must be careful. Also, phosphoric acid is generally found attached to fat and protein molecules, and must be separated by enzymes created by the kōji before being useful to the yeast. This demonstrates again the importance of properly making the kōji.

Obviously the source of water used in brewing is important. Rarely will ordinary tap water suffice. In fact, more kura get their water from wells than from any other source. The stable temperature of deep well water gives it consistency, although the individual qualities of a well will vary with depth and the surrounding terrain.

Many such wells are filled with water that has slowly filtered through local mountains. Other sources include underground rivers, above-ground rivers, springs, and lakes. Environmental changes have unfortunately rendered many water sources useless, but still many kura can brag about their local *meisui* (famous water) and how suited it is to saké brewing.

To some degree, water can be filtered and chemically altered to make it more suitable for saké brewing, and this is not uncommon. But there are definite limitations to this; if it isn't semidecent water to begin with, not much can be done to make it usable for saké brewing.

The various minerals combine to give water its taste as well as its texture. Based on this mineral content, water can seem either hard or soft to the palate, and is usually classified as *kōsui* (hard water) or *nansui* (soft water). Hard water allows a more vigorous fermentation to happen, and leads to clean, solid saké. Soft water often helps to bring about a saké that melts in to the palate, seductively drawing the various flavors with it. (Hiroshima saké is a fine example of the lovely results of brewing with soft water.)

Overall, Japan has slightly soft water when compared to other countries. Water types are generally the same throughout a region, and are sometimes listed on some of the more informative saké labels.

Yeast

Without yeast, there is no saké. Yeast eats the sugars produced when enzymes from the kōji chop up the starch in the rice, and gives off alcohol and carbon dioxide in return.

Until the early twentieth century, saké was made using naturally occurring yeast. The large tanks were left open to the surrounding environment, and yeast cells floating in the air would descend into the tank and — finding ideal conditions — begin fermenting. Eventually brewers would save the dormant yeast from the foam of particularly healthy and tasty batches and recultivate it for future use.

As time went on and technology improved, various strains of yeast were found to be superior. These were then cultivated on a large scale and made available to the industry as a whole. This is done by the Japan Saké Brewers' Association, and sold to brewers in small, hermetically sealed glass ampules, saving kura the trouble of maintaining their own stock in a sanitized environment.

Over the decades, more and more yeast strains were discovered. Some of these were clearly much better than their predecessors, others simply led to different types of saké. These various strains were assigned numeric names in the order they were discovered, i.e., Yeast No. 1, Yeast No. 2, all the way up to (at the time of this writing) Yeast No. 15. Each of these has its own characteristics and qualities.

Beyond these, many kura have their own proprietary yeast strains, discovered by and used only by them. There are also those that have been discovered by prefectural research institutes around Japan, and which are only made available to the breweries in those prefectures.

Yeast has quite a profound effect on the final fragrance and flavor of a saké. The various acids produced differ from yeast to yeast, and this will lead to different aromas, tastes, and textures. Some yeast will lead to dry, simple saké; other yeast will create fruity, ostentatious saké. And naturally, there is everything in between. Most breweries use a wide range of yeast strains, the choice of which for each tank depends on the grade of saké and other factors.

Beyond flavor and fragrance, yeast strains vary in other ways. Some are more robust than others and can survive more healthily in an alcohol-filled environment. Others have a longer life cycle, so that fermentation can proceed longer and more completely than usual. Still others might be particularly strong at lower temperatures, allowing more elegant and complex saké to be created.

Among the fifteen (or so) Brewers' Association yeasts, the first five are no longer used, as the acid they produced is a bit too overpowering for modern saké. No. 7 is the most commonly used yeast in the country, giving clean, mellow saké. It works at a higher temperature than most, allowing a faster fermentation. No. 9 is the most common ginjō yeast, and the fruity essences it helps create are enjoyed by ginjōshu fans everywhere.

No. 10 is more commonly seen used in the finer saké of the northern part of Japan as it suits the weather, rice, and water there more than other yeast types. It gives a more fine-grained flavor, with less acidity and can be used at lower temperatures.

Some of the more commonly seen prefectural yeasts include Akita Ryūka Kōbo (Akita) and Alps Kōbo (Nagano). Shizuoka, Fukushima, Kōchi, and Yamagata Prefectures also have well-known, character-laden yeast.

Dozens of strains of yeast are presently in use, and new ones are being isolated all the time. Often brewers seek "designer yeast" to go perfectly with their regional style, rice, and water. While it is certainly not that important for consumers to memorize all of this, the information is often provided (along with the other data given in this section) on the back labels of better saké.

◆ ◆ ◆

The terms and parameters described in this chapter are those that are most commonly provided by saké producers to consumers. As consumers' thirst for knowledge increases, more and more details are provided — at least by some brewers. Not all of these are so useful, although such data can certainly be quite interesting. Not only can they make choosing a saké more fun, but they remind us that saké is more than just a drink, and that saké brewing is an art and a craft that is always growing.

The taste and smell of the moromi or saké on any day tells the tōji how the final product will turn out and which adjustments are necessary.

CHAPTER FIVE

SAKÉ TASTING

*T*asting saké is not unlike tasting other fine beverages. While the basic nature of saké is different, and the array of flavors and aromas is certainly unique, the same senses and sensibilities are employed.

Saké is nothing if not subtle, and the transient nature of the tastes and smells makes for a fascinating tasting experience. Much affects what is perceived, and there are no hard-and-fast rules about tasting.

Just as in wine and other beverages, myriad things will have a very real effect on how a saké tastes and smells. Some of these are tangible, others less so. Temperature is one example.

Temperature

Temperature may have the most profound effect on a saké flavor profile. Every saké has different characteristics evident at different temperatures. This is due not solely to changes in the saké itself, but also to what the human tongue can sense at various temperatures. There is saké whose qualities are most enjoyable at warmer temperatures, saké best enjoyed slightly chilled, and saké that comes into its own at room temperature. And of course, personal tastes and preferences must be taken into consideration as well. In the end, each saké will have a different personality interacting with each person at every temperature. It's hardly simple.

The human tongue is apparently most sensitive at 21 degrees Celsius (70 degrees Fahrenheit). This is the temperature at which you could gather the most information about the flavor components of a saké. Although this may be appropriate for judging or looking for flaws, drinking *everything* at this temperature is certainly not the best way to enjoy saké.

The sweetness, or *amami*, of a saké is most detectable by the tongue when the saké is about the same temperature as our skin. But the perception of sweetness drops by 75 percent when the saké is overly chilled. Acidity, or sanmi, is somewhat understated in a chilled saké, but from 10 to 40 degrees Celsius (50 to 104 degrees Fahrenheit), the sensation of this flavor component does not change appreciably. Also, the warmer a saké is, the harder any bitter traces (*nigami*) can be to detect.

In short, there is no one best temperature for serving saké. *In general,* premium saké is served slightly chilled. What is slightly chilled? Again, it is not feasible to specify one single temperature, as every saké is different. But it will suffice to treat it like a white wine: a bit below room temperature works well, just out of the refrigerator is a bit too cold.

It can be extremely enjoyable to try a saké a bit on the chilled side, and observe it unfolding and changing as it slowly warms up. Different flavors and fragrances will appear, replacing others in a gentle, measured progression.

Until a few decades ago, almost all saké was invariably served warm. Although this may be perceived by some to be the "traditional" way to serve saké, it must be borne in mind that saké long ago was much rougher and less refined, fragrant, and complex than saké today. Only since the late 1960s or 1970s has saké worthy of being served chilled become widely available. (Although it existed long before that, few thought it economically viable.)

But today most better saké on the market is comprised of complex flavors and aromas that would be bludgeoned into nonexistence if heated. You would not be able to taste or smell precisely the things the brewer worked so hard to create. So personal preferences notwithstanding, most fine saké is better slightly chilled.

However, there are exceptions to this rule, and there are some premium saké that are wonderful when gently warmed. In fact, some old-timers will say that a truly good saké is one that can be enjoyed both warmed and chilled. Although a brewer may indicate ideal serving temperature on the bottle, there are no sure ways to know this other than experience culled from a willingness to experiment.

Looking at the various saké grades, daiginjō and ginjō fit into this better-off-chilled group, as does anything *unpasteurized* (namazaké). Honjōzō, with its overall lighter and smoother qualities, is often nice gently warmed. It is harder to generalize about junmaishu, as it can range from rugged and versatile to soft and gentle. As always, nothing can replace your own tasting experiences and inclinations.

Tasting Vessels

The choice of glass or cup will in many ways affect how a saké tastes as well. The shape of the cup or glass, its diameter, the thickness of the rim — all of these things will physically determine how a saké will hit your palate and in what way it will be distributed across your tongue. Contours in the cup will also affect how the aroma will be concentrated or diffused.

Traditionally (and still very commonly today), saké is drunk from small cups called *o-choko*, or slightly larger cups called *guinomi*, and is poured from tapered flasks known as *tokkuri*.

Larger cups never really came into common use because of (among other things) the deeply ingrained custom of people pouring saké for each other. This is seen as a sign of friendship and respect, and can be done more frequently when small glasses are used.

Also, Japan has a very rich tradition of pottery, with a diverse range of styles and manifestations. There are rough-hewn, unrefined styles and more refined, glazed wares as well.

The choice of o-choko or guinomi will have both measurable and intangible effects on any saké-tasting experience. This should not be underestimated. Epicurean delights like saké tasting should go beyond mere tastes and smells, and include tactile and visual appeal as well.

Wineglasses also work very well for saké, especially for more fragrant ginjō and daiginjō saké. Fluted stemware has never come into common use for saké in Japan, even in professional tasting competitions. But even if clear wineglasses may not offer the feel and appearance of traditional pottery, they are excellent for focusing and enhancing the delicate aromas and flavors of fine saké.

Simple tumblers and less ornate o-choko work just fine as well, and are certainly more readily available. These too will affect how a saké is perceived overall.

Finally, there are the small wooden boxes known as *masu*. While this is a traditional way of drinking saké, the flavors and fragrances of today's saké will be masked by the woody taste and smell of the box itself.

Naturally there is a whole host of other things that will affect how a saké tastes to you. How hungry you are, what kind of mood you are in, your current health conditions, even the people you are with will impart an effect on things. So will how dry or sweet the previous saké was (when tasting more than one), and of course the food you being served with the saké. The list is endless.

WHAT TO LOOK FOR IN SAKÉ

Saké drinking should be above all an enjoyable experience. As such, the main thing to pay attention to when tasting saké is simply whether or not it appeals to you.

There are several general aspects of a saké to look for in making this assessment. The first is balance. Pay attention to the fragrance, and notice whether it feels balanced with the flavor, both in terms of aromatic and flavor components, as well as in intensity. Next try to assess what specific flavors you perceive, related to aromas and flavors occurring in your everyday realm of smells and tastes. Finally, consider the more corporeal aspects of the saké: viscosity, weight, texture. Taking all of this in and appraising it within the context of your personal preferences is all there really is to tasting saké.

Flavor Components

Saké has countless flavor components. Only your imagination and vocabulary limit how they are expressed. Although saké may not have the breadth of flavor that some beverages have, it can have incredible depth and complexity.

A traditional approach — although somewhat limited in usefulness today — assesses saké in terms of its *go-mi*, or five flavors. These are *karami* (dryness), *nigami* (bitterness), *shibumi* (somewhere between astringency and tartness, but hard to translate directly), amami (sweetness), and sanmi (acidity). These give the mind something to objectively search for and assess.

This is just one method, and admittedly a bit outdated. Just as in wine, tasting involves looking for whatever fragrances and flavors you can perceive, no matter how wacky.

Nuts, herbs, fruits, rice, and grains are but a smattering of what can be found. Also important are textures: grainy mouth feel or smoothness, firm and crisp or absorbing, full and fat or narrow and clean. Saké can be refined or unkempt. Anything goes, if you like it personally.

Less desirable components include too thin a flavor, paper, burnt tones, roughness, and a whole host of unbalance and off flavors, things that just don't fit in well.

Aroma

Most often called the *kaori* in Japanese, the fragrance of a saké is just as much a part of the overall impression as the layers of flavor, if not more so. Aroma reveals countless things — everything from a solid sense of acidity, to a full rice sensation, to all kinds of herbs, fruits, and flowers. The nasty end of the aroma spectrum includes yeastiness, an overpowering presence of alcohol, rubber, mold, paper, and other unpleasant aspects indicative of improper care or processes gone awry.

Duration and impact are important to notice as well. Some saké has a fragrance that jumps right up at you; other saké is much more subtle and demure. Some has little or no fragrance at all. These aromas can last seconds only, or stay with the saké until the final sip. Although it is difficult to predict, some saké (usually that with a higher than average acidity) can benefit from a bit of decanting, as the fragrance is coaxed into revealing itself.

Balance

Perhaps most important overall aspect is balance. Balance in the aroma, balance in the flavor, and also balance between these two. A lively fragrance and an overly simple flavor are not well matched, nor are a subdued aroma and a wild flavor. A decent saké will have a balance in the intensity and elements of the aroma and the flavor.

TASTING TERMINOLOGY

When tasting any beverage, we generally get an overall impression, do some internal filing and comparing, and decide whether or not we like it. Some people are easily able to tie these impressions to memories and some are not. Coming up with an objective description using concrete words often allows us to remember these initial impressions later. We then create a base of knowledge and experience that makes it easier to determine our own preferences.

Naturally, the Japanese language includes a large collection of descriptive words for tasting saké. However, many of them do not translate into English well, or at all in some cases.

It is definitely a good idea to first note your taste impressions in your own native tongue, especially when learning to appreciate and discern different types of saké. These are the impressions that will surface most quickly, offer themselves most readily, and be most closely tied to how you sense the flavors and smells. It also helps immensely to record these impressions in writing.

At the same time, it can be both educational and fun to see how saké is assessed in Japanese. Also, some of the terms represent concepts that may not have an English single-word equivalent, and may be worth borrowing from time to time.

Some General Terms

Looking first at some of the more general terms, dry saké is referred to as *karakuchi*, and sweet saké is known as *amakuchi*, although the adjectives *karai* and *amai* can be used respectively as well. A light and refined saké is referred to as *tanrei*, and *tanrei karakuchi* is a commonly encountered description of the light, dry saké so popular in Japan.

Hōjun refers to a mellow, perhaps mildly rich saké. *Nigiyaka* saké is lively, active, and playful, implying *freshness* and an abundance of competing flavors and impressions. Heavy saké is *omoi* saké and light saké is *karui* saké.

Palate

The way a saké strikes the palate is known as the *kuchiatari*. This could be soft, firm, lively, or quiet, but is an important point in assessing saké style. A saké that hits your tongue and spreads like a wave crashing on the beach, infiltrating every nook and cranny of your palate, is described as *fukurami ga ii.*

A well-rounded saké — one with lots of flavor components and elements that help the flavor feel complete — can be described as *marumi ga aru*, while one that is simpler and cleaner, with not as much happening and perhaps fewer discernible individual flavor components, may be referred to as *hosoi*, meaning narrow. Such saké is prized by some, and its compact flavor can also be referred to as *katai*, or firm.

Koku is a quality indicating a mature, settled, almost earthy touch to saké. This useful term does not translate into English words very well, and needs to be experienced to be fully understood.

Torotto describes the feeling of saké that quickly melts into your palate, while *tsūn-to-kuru* describes a sharp blast of flavor, often from a high acidity or higher alcohol content. This term can be used in both flattering and critical ways. *Shibui* can describe a saké that is somewhere between astringent and tart, but it can also have the wonderful meaning of having all the essentials but nothing superfluous.

The finish of a saké — the way it disappears or lingers on the throat and palate — is often scrutinized, and is known as the *nodogoshi*. When a saké vanishes quickly from the realm of your senses in a particularly pleasant way, it is said to be *kire ga ii.*

To describe a saké that is light and pretty, the word *kirei* is often used. A less specific but fun term to describe a saké that is just plain good is *umai*!

Fragrance

A vast number of words describe the kaori, or fragrance of a saké. These are often simple fruit, flower, or ricelike sensations, with esters, earthy tones, and herbal notes as well. That unique aroma associated with ginj–oshu in general is known as a ginjōka, although this is a somewhat broad term.

Critical Terms

Naturally, terms exist for more critical appraisals as well. A saké that is cloying, with too much of any one component such as sweetness, is often called *kudoi*. Quirks or strange qualities that don't seem to belong are called *kuse*, a particularly subjective term.

A heavy saké is referred to as *omoi*, and too strong a flavor is *koi*. The opposite, a thin flavor, would be known as *usui*. *Zatsumi* is a commonly encountered term that refers to strange off flavors that detract from the overall quality of a saké. A saké that is just plain bad is called *mazui*, but hopefully you'll never need to use this word! If a saké seems to have suffered from improper or excessive aging, it is called *hinette-iru*, and an old-saké smell is known as a *hineka*.

Umami

Finally, umami is a term that has worked its way into wine language as well, and is often seen as is in English. Umami refers to a hard-to-pinpoint tastiness or goodness, more intuitively sensed than overtly tasted. In an effort to convey the concept, consider that chocolate, scallops, mushrooms, and Parmesan cheese have great umami, whereas fresh greens and white bread do not. Umami is another perception that is best grasped through actual tasting.

The list could go on endlessly, but the best way to learn to convey your own impressions about saké is to taste a wide range of styles. But avoid getting overly involved in all this. Simply enjoying saké is the real point, and too much intellectualizing cannot contribute too much to that end.

HEATING SAKÉ

In spite of previous admonitions that fine saké be served slightly chilled, warmed saké definitely has its appeal, especially in the colder months.

Warmed saké in general is known as *kanzake*, or the honorific *o-kan*. A few vague and overlapping terms define just how warm a saké is. *Nurukan* (lukewarm) ranges from just above room temperature to about 40 degrees Celsius (104 degrees Fahrenheit). *Kan* (warm) picks up somewhere around there and runs to perhaps 55 degrees Celsius (130 degrees Fahrenheit). *Atsukan* (piping hot) is anything hotter than that.

Perhaps the most interesting term, as well as a fine all-around serving temperature, is *hito-hada* (which literally means a person's skin, but suggests body temperature). While it may be a bit tepid for some, saké warmed to only this temperature can be very enjoyable indeed.

Most restaurants serve hot saké from a machine, and getting them to warm it separately for you may be like pulling teeth. Saké specialty pubs may warm it gently and properly for you, but many will not bother with warming saké at all. Fortunately warming it at home is a painless process.

When heating saké, perhaps the one thing to avoid is overheating. Once a saké has been overheated, it never seems to cool down to what it once was. Balance and character are usually destroyed, and the texture will end up syrupy and cloying.

The easiest way to warm saké is to place a vessel in a small pan of water, then heat the water and saké in the flask together.

A proper tokkuri flask is a good vessel to use, although it is by no means absolutely necessary. Its tapered top will retain the heat longer.

Pick the tokkuri up by the neck and swirl the saké in it every so often to keep the temperature distribution even. Sip the saké from time to time until it is just right for your taste.

Another alternative is to microwave the saké. But as strange as it might seem, microwaving does take a bit of the zing out.

There are small thermometers available for checking the temperature of the saké as you heat it, should you prefer a scientific approach over an empirical one.

Although there is no hard medical evidence to support it, warm saké seems to hit many people harder. The magical glow of the evening as well as the not-so-magical glow of the next morning both seem intensified. Be careful!

OFFICIAL SAKÉ TASTINGS

Each spring, soon after the brewing season has ended, the saké-brewing industry holds its *shinshu kanpyōkai* (new saké appraisal competitions). Japan is the only country in the world that sponsors government-run tasting competitions for its indigenous alcoholic beverages.

There are normally eleven regional events in the first round, followed by a national event. This very prestigious industry event is run by the Saké Brewing Research Center, which is partially funded by the Ministry of Taxation. (In Japan, as in any country, alcoholic beverages are strictly taxed. As such, the government keeps close tabs on how much is brewed at each kura so as to get their due on every drop.)

Until the early 1990s, the kyūbetsu seido grading system mentioned earlier was still in use, in which saké was ranked as Tokkyū (special class), Ikkyū (first class), or the default category

Nikyū (second class). To assess these somewhat dubious grades, the tax department maintained a staff of official tasters and graders.

When this system was abolished, the masterful palates and noses of the tax department remained. Today they are employed in assessing gold and silver prizes to those saké that are deemed worthy at the end of each brewing season. Although such prizes have no effect on the taxes assessed (as the now-defunct special class and first class designations did), significant prestige is indeed associated with being a *kinshō jushōshu*, a gold medal-winning saké.

Saké submitted to this contest is specially brewed for competition, and rarely makes its way into the market (and when it does, it is understandably fairly pricey). It is somewhat exaggerated in its profile, and very focused on the qualities needed to win a gold. Although it is interesting, usually one glass is plenty, with most people preferring more relaxed, well-rounded saké.

These tasting competitions are of course done blind; no labels are exposed and the judges have no way of knowing what they are tasting. The number of gold and silver prizes is not strictly limited and varies slightly from year to year.

After the results have been tabulated and are about to be announced, members of the public are allowed in to taste the saké as well. This is both frenetic and fun. Fortunately at this time the labels are exposed and the prizewinners are indicated.

A similar event is held in the autumn. This, however, does not hold the same significance or prestige as the spring event.

Some insist that since such contests do not use saké actually on the market, there is not much meaning behind them. But these events do in fact demonstrate the skill of the brewer in being able to precisely create saké that conforms to specific parameters while still maintaining individuality.

Of even larger importance is the saké produced by a kura for consumption by the average consumer. This is a very real standard of quality for consumers, as it is more grounded in reality for most of us.

ON STORING SAKÉ

Properly storing and caring for saké, both before and after opening a bottle, greatly affects its quality and freshness. The enemies are the same as those for other fine beverages: excessive oxygen, light, and high temperatures.

In short, saké should be stored at cool temperatures, and kept out of strong direct light. Most saké does not need to be refrigerated, but refrigeration certainly cannot hurt.

Namazaké, unpasteurized saké, is an exception to this. Namazaké must be kept quite cold or the chances of it going bad are high; enzymes kick in to make the saké yeasty, cloying, and way out of balance.

Saké is not generally aged, but rather consumed within a year of brewing. This does not mean that it will go bad that quickly, only that it will slowly begin to change into something different. As saké sits on the shelf, it becomes a bit more well-rounded, but it can also become heavier and more concentrated in flavor. It will darken, and may take on a musty touch as well. This is not always entirely unpleasant, and many people enjoy saké like this.

However, the rule of thumb is best stated thusly: If you want to taste a saké *the way the brewer wanted you to taste it*, drink it soon (within six months to a year) and keep it cool in the meantime. The colder it is kept, the more slowly it will change in the bottle.

Finally, after a bottle of saké has been opened, it should be consumed as soon as possible. After opening, saké, like wine, will begin to oxidize. The flavor and fragrance will begin to fade, and the saké will start to lose its finer edges. The more delicate and subtle the flavor is, the more susceptible the saké is to deterioration.

There are exceptions; not all saké goes downhill so fast. Some saké seems fine a couple of weeks after having been opened. But in general, be on the safe side and drink it within a few days.

◆ ◆ ◆

From temperature to terminology, from fragrance to flavor, tasting saké is above all very enjoyable. Although this chapter presented things as they are done and viewed in Japan, there are no rules, and the only right way to taste and assess is the one that works best for each individual.

CHAPTER SIX

THE PEOPLE OF THE SAKÉ BREWING WORLD

*T*he world of saké brew masters, known as tōji, and the craftsmen that work under them, referred to as kurabito, or "people of the kura," is one of rich history and culture, laden with idiosyncrasies and curious customs.

Rarely does the owner of a brewery actually do any brewing. Although there are a few cases of this today, it was all but unheard of until recent years. Instead, the craftsmen brewing were most often farmers from the snowy, backwoods countryside of Japan. As there was little to do after the rice had been harvested and the snow came, a wonderfully symbiotic relationship developed between such farmers and saké brewers that only needed skilled help in the winter, during the brewing season.

Kurabito would leave their families and homes behind each autumn and travel to saké kura to live and work for the next six months. Very often, they would travel in teams, along with their leader and boss, the tōji of the kura.

Although often prestigious and rewarding, the life of kurabito and tōji was indeed a harsh one. Not only were they away from their families for half of each year, but the work was hard and cold. Beyond that, the hierarchy was strict and feudal, with the tōji at the top and everyone else in a clear rank below that. Until recently kurabito were always men, and women were not even allowed to set foot in the kura. Although kurabito and tōji have come from all regions of Japan, agricultural demographics dictated that some regions had more farmers available for such work. With all those kurabito and tōji returning to the region in the summer, guilds, in which techniques were shared and passed on to younger apprentices, emerged in each region. These guilds center around the tōji, and are known as *tōji ryūha*. Each has developed their own tricks of the trade and methods that often impart a discernible quality to the saké they brew. Tōji ryūha are teeming with history and tradition and, although they are not today as important as they once were, they are a vital part of the culture of the saké world.

Historically there were several dozen of these guilds, spread out around Japan. Some had hundreds of tōji members, others but a few. Many of these no longer exist, as the last member of the guild retired or passed away with either no successor or no kura at which to brew. Others are still strong in numbers.

Some of the larger tōji ryūha and their original locations are:

- *Nanbu Tōji* (Iwate Prefecture)
- *Echigō Tōji* (Niigata Prefecture)
- *Tanba Tōji* (Hyogo Prefecture)
- *Tajima Tōji* (Hyogo Prefecture)
- *Nōto Tōji* (Ishikawa Prefecture)
- *Hiroshima Tōji* (Hiroshima Prefecture)
- *Sannai Tōji* (Akita Prefecture)
- *Izumo Tōji* (Shimane Prefecture)
- *Bitchū Tōji* (Okayama Prefecture)

The names of each guild correspond to the ancient names for the respective regions.

Originally tōji and kurabito tended to work at breweries within or close to their home prefecture when possible. But as of late, as many of the smaller guilds have vanished, tōji are traveling farther and farther from home.

The largest and most significant of these tōji ryūha have always been the Nanbu, Echigō, and Tanba guilds. This is true even in modern times.

Today, however, things have changed quite a bit. As the number of kura brewing saké has dropped significantly over the years, so have the number of tōji. With the exception of the Nanbu Tōji, whose organized education program has kept their numbers constant, all the others have significantly fewer members, and many have altogether vanished.

The system of having one head brewer from one of the established guilds has also changed significantly. More and more breweries use locally hired people, not craftsmen from afar. Today it is not uncommon to have both the tōji and the kurabito come from nearby, with various arrangements made to accommodate the grueling working hours of the winter. Unheard of long ago, one or two days off a week during the brewing season is now a common part of the lives of many kurabito. Also, women are commonly found working in the breweries these days, with many breweries employing female kurabito, and even several women tōji in existence. This would have been unthinkable only a few decades ago.

Many of these changes were necessary due to societal changes. Fewer and fewer young people were interested in the harsh working conditions and total commitment necessary to brew saké. Most would rather take a desk job in the big city and go out on Friday nights. Also, what few experienced tōji and kurabito from the farther regions were left have become quite advanced in age, with almost no one to replace them from the guild. So while the older, traditional system is still in place to some degree at the majority of kura, the breath of fresh air of new tradition being born is evident everywhere.

There is more than just historical and cultural significance to the various tōji guilds. Each of these guilds excels at making certain styles of saké; techniques subtly differ as well. For students of saké — and not mere tipplers — a study of this aspect of the saké world will prove fascinating.

State of the Industry

The brewing industry has risen and fallen countless times over the years, decimated by wars, earthquakes, and poor economies. Saké production peaked in 1973 and has been on the decline ever since, due in a large part to the introduction of beer, wine, and other alternatives.

Long ago the battle was more often between the large mass producers of saké and the smaller brewers from the countryside struggling to survive in their shadow. Now things are hard everywhere, and each year a few more breweries cease operation.

Yet, paradoxically, better saké is being brewed more now than ever before. While consumption overall is on the decline, consumption of *premium* saké is actually on the increase, albeit slightly. Sadly saké like this is not as profitable, and the industry continues to sag despite how wonderful the product is.

All is not lost, however, and the status of the industry is expected to again stabilize. While a few more kura may disappear, the market will find its balance again, and demand for fine saké will likely continue to grow at its slow if measured pace.

Traditional Measurements

Most saké comes in awkwardly sized 1.8 liter bottles, or alternatively, smaller 720 milliliter bottles. For those that have wondered why they did not use an even two liters, or 750 milliliters like the rest of the world, the answer lies in the traditional measurements of Japan.

It all starts with the masu, a small cedar box that saké is occasionally served in, particularly in ceremonies and around the new year.

Originally the masu was used as a measurement for rice, with rice being a currency of sorts in Shogunate-run Japan centuries ago. Both taxes and stipends for retainers were often paid with rice, and the masu was the basic unit of measure.

Why folks began using the wooden box to drink saké is not totally clear, but it is interesting to note that until about eighty years ago, saké was brewed and stored in vessels of the same wood (*sugi,* Japanese cedar) used to make masu.

One masu holds just about 180 milliliters, and this became the standard size of a single serving. This volume of liquid is known as one *gō*, and saké is still priced in pubs in terms of *ichi-gō* (one gō) or *ni gō* (two gō) flagons.

As a natural extension of this, the 1.8 liter bottles came into being because they are exactly ten gō. The 720 milliliter bottles, known as *yongō* (four gō) bottles, being four servings — two glasses each for two people — also start to make sense.

The 1.8 liter bottles are known as *isshō-bin* (one *shō* bottles) and ten *shō* equal one *to*. The large glass container holding this 18-liter volume is known as an *itto-bin*, and is used today (to help separate the very best from the best) when pressing saké in one of the traditional methods. Since each of these 18-liter bottles will taste ever-so-slightly different, brewers can earmark different bottles for contests, or for sale as top-class saké.

Taking a step back and looking at a small scale, one tenth of one gō is known as a *shaku.* Mention of this 18-milliliter unit is rare, but it does exist, for the record. Since such thimble-sized bottles would be a bit impractical, single shaku containers do not exist, of course. However, often at saké pubs prices are given for *hasshaku*, or eight shaku, which is but eight-tenths of a full masu.

The wooden casks known as taru that are ceremoniously opened with a hammer at festivities in Japan can hold anywhere from one *to* (then called an *itto-daru*) to the more commonly seen four *to* (*yon-to daru*). There are other sizes as well.

On an even larger scale, ten to are known as one *koku*. One koku is therefore 180 liters, which would also be equal in volume to 100 isshō-bin. The number of koku brewed is the traditional basic unit of production output of a saké brewery.

Although people do naturally speak of the number of kiloliters a kura brews, it is very common in the industry to hear talk of the *koku-sū*, or number of koku that is brewed. Once one gets a feel for evaluating the size and capacity of a kura in terms of koku, it becomes hard to go back to thinking in terms of kiloliters.

As a vague point of reference, a kura making less than one thousand koku is quite small (although there are countless kura of this scale). Ten thousand koku, while not huge, is large and stable in terms of production.

The yearly production of a brewery is generally not available on bottles may be of interest to those that enjoy touring saké breweries, searching for those that brew very little. Knowing the scale of a kura can add to the sense of romanticism — or detract from it, as the case may be.

Although this system of measurement may not be the most convenient for number crunching, it is firmly in place and shows no sign of changing. These measures are at least interesting as a vestige of centuries past, and the long and rich history of the world of saké.

PART TWO

その二
銘酒百選

CHAPTER SEVEN

RECOMMENDED
NIHONSHU SELECTIONS

*C*onsidering the large number or kura in Japan (about 1,600), picking one hundred or so saké (nihonshu) to recommend can be quite a daunting task. First of all, there is no way anyone could taste every saké in the country in a reasonable amount of time and live to give an exhaustive summary. There is such a range of styles, and so much good stuff out there that choosing even as many as one hundred seems limiting. Combine this with the fact that things change at least somewhat from year to year, and you get an idea of the limitations imposed upon someone wishing to introduce others to the joys of drinking saké.

The list presented here is by no means comprehensive. There are very likely some saké you have tasted or had recommended to you, especially smaller local brands, that are not mentioned here. Also, many famous names and saké from larger breweries are not included; this is not because their saké is not recommendable, but rather because it is so easy to find. Try the saké of big brands and easy-to-find larger kura; if you like it, great.

An attempt has been made to represent all styles and regions fairly. Junmaishu, honjōzō, ginjōshu, and other types are all represented, as are light saké, heavy saké, dry, sweet, acidic, and soft. Some of the saké recommended here are easy to find; others call for a good bit of digging around. Although not every prefecture has been represented, most regions of Japan have.

Just to make things difficult, kura sometimes change the labels used for a particular brew, or use more than one design for the same saké, depending on the season, or slight variations in the saké itself. Thus, the labels pictured here may not be the same as those found in your local liquor shop, so look carefully. On the other hand, once you get a handle on the name of the kura, you may find other offerings from the same brewery that are worth trying. Keep these points in mind when shopping or ordering.

A saké kura usually (but not always) has one *meigara*, or brand label. Under this meigara are sold various types of saké, like a junmaishu or a daiginjō. On top of this, they may make more than one saké of the same type. For example, they may have one junmai ginjō saké made from one kind of rice, and another junmai ginjō made from another kind of rice. To differentiate, they give each of these a different name.

Thus, when looking for a saké, you may have to keep the kura name, the meigara, the name of a particular brew within this meigara, and the type of saké (junmaishu, ginjōshu, etc.) in mind.

The saké listings appear in geographical order, beginning with such northern areas as Hokkaido and Amori and then progressing south.

They are laid out in this section as follows.

男 山 「生酛」

MEIGARA
(BRAND NAME)

Otokoyama

"Kimoto" • *junmaishu*

Hokkaido

KOJIRUSHI • TYPE
(SUB-BRAND)

PREFECTURE
WHERE SAKÉ
IS MADE

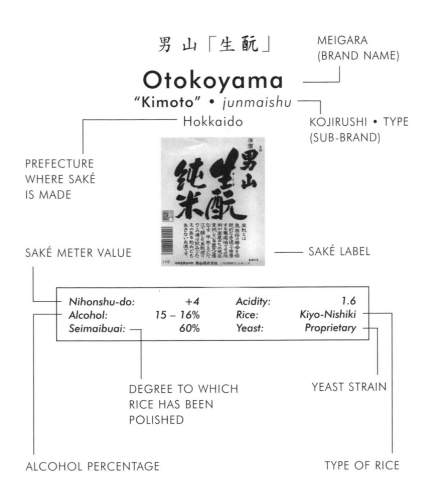

SAKÉ METER VALUE

SAKÉ LABEL

Nihonshu-do:	+4	Acidity:	1.6
Alcohol:	15 – 16%	Rice:	Kiyo-Nishiki
Seimaibuai:	60%	Yeast:	Proprietary

DEGREE TO WHICH
RICE HAS BEEN
POLISHED

YEAST STRAIN

ALCOHOL PERCENTAGE

TYPE OF RICE

Otokoyama
"Kimoto" • *junmaishu*
Hokkaido

Nihonshu-do:	+4	Acidity:	1.6
Alcohol:	15 – 16%	Rice:	Kiyo-Nishiki
Seimaibuai:	60%	Yeast:	Proprietary

There are several saké with the meigara Otokoyama, but this one from Hokkaido is probably the most famous. It is very light and dry, with a crispness to the overall flavor, but it is a bit softer than most dry saké. Soon after it hits your tongue, there is a sharpness supplanted by a slight bitterness. The flavor evaporates from your tongue and throat quite quickly.

田 酒

Denshu
Junmaishu
Aomori Prefecture

Nihonshu-do:	+4	Acidity:	1.7
Alcohol:	15.6%	Rice:	Hanafubuki
Seimaibuai:	58%	Yeast:	Number 9

This kura is not very big, but fortunately Denshu is not so difficult to find. Both the flavor and the fragrance are ricelike, quite fruity, with not a lot of wild elements. A relaxed and calm saké that will suffer from excessive chilling, yet neither is it suited to too much warming.

OTHER OFFERINGS: Another nihonshu produced by this company (at a different location) goes by the name of Kikuizumi. The name Denshu has been around since 1974, and only junmaishu is produced under this name. Kikuizumi daiginjō is a complex brew with a fruity fragrance that is quite popular locally, although not as easily found as Denshu.

桃川

Momokawa
Tokubetsu honjōzō
Aomori Prefecture

Nihonshu-do:	+2	Acidity:	1.5
Alcohol:	15.5%	Rice:	Hanafubuki
Seimaibuai:	58%	Yeast:	Number 9

Overall a gentle and soft saké, with a mild sweetness lingering in the background, almost as an afterthought. The flavors blend in and play off each other in a masterful way. The fragrance is gentle and mildly reminiscent of fruit.

OTHER OFFERINGS: Momokawa has a wonderfully balanced daiginjōshu as well. This kura is also brewing saké in the United States (since 1997).

Hiraizumi
Yamahai junmaishu
Akita Prefecture

Nihonshu-do:	+4	Acidity:	1.9
Alcohol:	15.2%	Rice:	Miyama-Nishiki
Seimaibuai:	58%	Yeast:	Number 7

This saké is a bit cleaner and more refined than the average yamahai-shikomi. There is an earthy aspect to the flavor that is contrasted nicely by a solid acidity. The flavor hangs around for a while without becoming cloying. The fragrance is somewhat unique for nihonshu, but it seems to fit in well with the rest of the saké's attributes.

Hiraizumi is the third oldest kura still operating in Japan, having been founded in 1487.

刈 穂「六 舟」

Karihō
"Rokushū" • *nama ginjōshu*
Akita Prefecture

Nihonshu-do:	+5	Acidity:	1.4
Alcohol:	15.5%	Rice:	Miyama-Nishiki, Toyo-Nishiki
Seimaibuai:	55%	Yeast:	Number 9

Rokushū has a light fragrance that is a little hard to find, but one that is pleasantly light and settled. It seems to tie in well with the flavor. It hits your palate lightly and spreads out, melting along the way. It is a bit sweeter than the nihonshu-do might indicate, but its softness amplifies this sensation. It is nice chilled, but maintains its balance at room temperature as well.

OTHER OFFERINGS: Kariho also makes a yamahai junmaishu labeled Chō Karakuchi (super dry) that makes very good kanzake (warmed saké).

喜久水「縄文能代」

Kikusui
"Jōmon Noshiro" • *ginjōshu*
Akita Prefecture

Nihonshu-do:	+4	Acidity:	1.3
Alcohol:	15.3%	Rice:	Miyama-Nishiki
Seimaibuai:	55%	Yeast:	Number 901

The nose is light and soft, with a touch of marshmallow in it; but rather faint, so you have to look for it. This saké is soft and airy as it hits the palate, with a good mouth feel that doesn't distract. This sensation spreads into a gentle sweetness that melts onto your palate just before evaporating rather quickly from your tongue.

南部美人

Nanbu Bijin
Junmai ginjōshu
Iwate Prefecture

Nihonshu-do:	+2	Acidity:	1.3
Alcohol:	15.8	Rice:	Toyonishiki
Seimaibuai:	55%	Yeast:	Number 9

Saké from the northern part of the island of Honshū traditionally has a heavier, sweeter taste. It has been said that, in olden times, drinking a glass of saké from this region was equivalent to eating three bowls of rice. Although these saké have slowly given way to the homogenized, less distinctive flavor profile that today's consumers seem to prefer, some differences can still be noted. One saké typifying this style and region is Nanbu Bijin.

This saké has a definite ricelike flavor, full-bodied and heavy. As the nihonshu-do of +2 indicates, it is just slightly on the sweet side, but its richness seems to amplify this sensation. The fragrance is just as solid, with very little fruitiness or alcohol apparent.

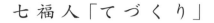

Shichifukujin
"Tezukuri" • *daiginjōshu*
Iwate Prefecture

Nihonshu-do:	+7	Acidity:	1.3
Alcohol:	15.8%	Rice:	Yamada-Nishiki, Sasa-Nishiki
Seimaibuai:	50%	Yeast:	Number 10

As with other saké from this region, Shichifukujin is full-bodied, with an unmistakable rice presence in the flavor. While maintaining this connection to the traditional style of saké for the region, it is still a bit lighter than average. The full body makes it very satisfying, and a touch of fruitiness in the fragrance brightens the impression of the saké in general. The flavor is slightly dry, although this depends on serving temperature.

Its strength is its simplicity; it does not have a complex flavor profile, but rather a straightforward one that is easy to appreciate. Moderately chilled seems to be the best serving temperature, but do not hesitate to try it gently warmed.

浜千鳥

Hamachidori
Junmai ginjōshu
Iwate Prefecture

Nihonshu-do:	+2	Acidity:	1.3
Alcohol:	15 – 16%	Rice:	Miyama-Nishiki
Seimaibuai:	45%	Yeast:	Number 9

This saké has a wonderful rice presence, and a texture to its flavor that is hard to find elsewhere. The fragrance is gently sweet and rice-based, and draws you in to the rest of the saké. The flavor itself is soft, with a low acid presence. Soon after it hits your palate, however, it takes on an interesting texture, as the different flavors vie for the attention of your taste buds.

This saké's strength is in its texture, and the way it runs around your mouth seems to amplify this, though not to the point of being cloying.

Uragasumi
Honjōzō
Miyagi Prefecture

Nihonshu-do:	±0	Acidity:	1.3
Alcohol:	15.2%	Rice:	Toyo-Nishiki
Seimaibuai:	55%	Yeast:	Proprietary

This is a readily available and very versatile saké. It is not markedly distinctive in any single attribute, but it is consistently impressive, in the sense that it never fails to satisfy.

This honjōzō is just on the sweet side of neutral, with an acidity in the flavor that seems higher than the 1.3 would indicate. The nose is faint but present, and seems to fit in with the rest of the flavors involved. This gentle saké is good at slightly cooler than room temperature, rather than thoroughly chilled. It is also a fine choice for atsukan (heated saké) die-hards, but don't overdo it!

十四代「無濾過中取り」

Jūyondai
"Muroka Nakadori" • *junmaishu*
Yamagata Prefecture

Nihonshu-do:	+2	Acidity:	1.4
Alcohol:	16 – 17%	Rice:	Miyama-Nishiki
Seimaibuai:	55%	Yeast:	Number 9

This saké has a balance and solidity to it that is extremely satisfying. The nose is just a touch spicy-fruity, but it somehow ties into the rice flavor and entices you to taste it. In fact, the balance of all flavors demands your attention. It is ever-so-slightly on the sweet side, but in a way that will attract even karakuchi (dry) saké fans. The finish is crisp, without disappearing too fast. This particular saké is unfiltered (muroka).

OTHER OFFERINGS: There are several ginjōshu available from Jūyondai using various rices — all are superb.

出 羽 桜 「桜 花」

Dewazakura
"Ōka" • *ginjōshu namazaké*
Yamagata Prefecture

Nihonshu-do:	+5	Acidity:	1.2
Alcohol:	15.5%	Rice:	Miyama-Nishiki, others
Seimaibuai:	50%	Yeast:	Ogawa

The nose of this unpasteurized saké has a fruitiness that really jumps out at you, young in a way that a wine or beer may be young; the flavors contrast each other with a brashness that one senses may mellow with time. It has a fairly full flavor that doesn't disappear too quickly. In short, it is quite easy to drink, especially mildly chilled. The alcohol is just a bit lower than average, making it too easy to drink just a bit more.

The name Ōka means cherry blossoms; so look for it in early April when the cherry trees are in bloom and this saké is especially easy to find.

OTHER OFFERINGS: Dewazakura has several fine offerings, including a junmai ginjōshu.

くどき上手

Kudoki Jōzu

Junmai ginjōshu
Yamagata Prefecture

Nihonshu-do:	+1	Acidity:	1.2
Alcohol:	16.6%	Rice:	Miyama-Nishiki
Seimaibuai:	40%	Yeast: Ogawa Number 101	

If nothing else, this saké should win a prize for having an interesting name. Translated roughly as "pick-up artist," its name never fails to bring a smile, for one reason or another.

Fortunately, there is much more to this saké than its name. It is a light and balanced saké that is actually quite distinct. The flavor is clean, with a soft fruitiness. The nose is quite fruity and flowery, often with a solid essence of apples, especially in the finish. The balance, however, is not sacrificed. A good example of a "feminine" saké. The finer qualities of Kudoki Jōzu are brought out by mild chilling, and not as much by higher serving temperatures.

OTHER OFFERINGS: This saké is more subdued than some of its higher-priced Kudoki Jōzu daiginjō siblings, of which there are several, all highly recommended.

栄 光 富 士

Eikō Fuji
Nama junmaishu
Yamagata Prefecture

Nihonshu-do:	+4	Acidity:	1.4
Alcohol:	15.5	Rice:	Miyama-Nishiki
Seimaibuai:	64%	Yeast:	Number 10

Eikō Fuji is a fresh, no-nonsense saké with an unmistakable distinction. Clean is a word that describes it quite well. The nose is not very pronounced at all; it's quite faint in fact. But the proof is in the flavor. It does not have an excessive amount of body or mouth feel, yet there is a solidness and balance to it. Although it is a junmaishu, there is not a lot of acidity detectable in the flavor. This namazaké is quite lively, with an eye-opening flavor that is not easily forgotten.

OTHER OFFERINGS: Eikō Fuji also makes several other excellent saké, including a ginjōshu called Yuki no Furu Machiwo, and an excellent daiginjō called Kozakaya no Hitoriyogari.

大山

Ōyama

Tokubetsu junmaishu
Yamagata Prefecture

Nihonshu-do:	+8	Acidity:	1.45
Alcohol:	15.3%	Rice:	Sasa-Nishiki, Sekkajō
Seimaibuai:	60%	Yeast:	Yamagata KA

Ōyama can be both simple and interesting at the same time. Generally dry and solid, it has a dependably full flavor. The top part of the aggregation of flavor elements melts away soon after sipping, but the bottom tends to stay with you for a while. This saké is dry at first, but changes and fades leaving a thread of sweetness in the trail. Soft and gentle throughout.

初 孫

Hatsumago
Honjōzō
Yamagata Prefecture

Nihonshu-do:	+2	Acidity:	1.4
Alcohol:	15.5%	Rice:	Yoneshiro
Semaibuai:	58%	Yeast:	Number 9,
			Number 10

This saké is made using the labor-intensive kimoto method of creating moto, yeast starter, something this kura excels at. The overall impression is definitely dry and clean, but there are layers of hidden flavor elements waiting to be discovered. A fine choice for kanzake, or warm saké, as it will be quite smooth and perhaps all too drinkable at warmer temperatures. The label is (no surprise here) silver; an easy-to-find saké.

Hatsumago is well known for consistency of quality, as evident by their remarkable ability to win a gold medal almost every single year in the new saké tasting competitions

香梅

Kōbai
Ginjōshu
Yamagata Prefecture

Nihonshu-do:	+4	Acidity:	1.2
Alcohol:	15% – 16%	Rice:	Yamada-Nishiki
Semaibuai:	50%	Yeast:	Number 9

Although not large by volume-of-production standards, this kura runs a flagship shop in Tokyo where one can sample all their saké. This particular saké is wonderfully complex, with chameleon-like layers. A faint essence of strawberries, cherries, and even grapes blends into a gentle but anchored fragrance. This saké has a rich and grainy taste-profile that hits your palate with gentle assertiveness and kindly requests your attention. Full-bodied but clean, with a perfectly balanced acidity. Good alone, or with mildly salty vegetable dishes. May not work as well with oily food. Best served cool or cold.

Sharaku
Junmai daiginjōshu
Fukushima Prefecture

Nihonshu-do:	+3	Acidity:	1.5
Alcohol:	15 – 16%	Rice:	Miyama-Nishiki
Semaibuai:	50%	Yeast:	Number 9

Sharaku offers a sensation that spreads all the way across your tongue, dripping little bits and pieces of flavor along the way. Named after the nineteenth-century woodblock print artist who mysteriously disappeared after an illustrious ten-month career, this saké has a distinction that you'll not tire of. The fragrance is well balanced, and has quite a bit of staying power; it doesn't seem to fade away as happens with some saké. It is full-bodied, and slightly on the sweet side. There is very little acidic sharpness in the flavor. The finish is dryer than when it first hits your palate, and there is a slight lingering sweetness that is not in the least bit cloying. Best at room temperature or slightly cooler.

大七「極上生一本」

Daishichi
"Gokujō Ki Ippon" • *Junmai daiginjōshu*
Fukushima Prefecture

Nihonshu-do:	+3	Acidity:	1.3
Alcohol:	16%	Rice:	Yamada-Nishiki
Semaibuai:	38%	Yeast:	Proprietary

Fairly unique as far as daiginjō flavor profiles go. It's very clean and balanced, but the bitter and tart elements of the flavor seem more prominent, making this saké better at room temperature, or even lukewarm, rather than chilled. It was the first daiginjōshu to be made using the kimoto method.

OTHER OFFERINGS: This saké comes in two packages — a silver-label version pressed in the normal way, and a gold-label version pressed with a fune (a wooden box used for pressing saké the old, laborious way). Also, Daishichi junmaishu is an easy-to-drink brew that has a very soft nose, and a neutral flavor that melts well and lingers just a bit.

開 富 男 山

Kaitō Otokoyama

Junmaishu
Fukushima Prefecture

Nihonshu-do:	+1	Acidity:	1.4
Alcohol:	15.3%	Rice:	Gohyakumangoku
Semaibuai:	62%	Yeast:	Number 9

The overall impression of this saké is that it is fairly soft and pillowy, absorbing into your palate in its own good time. No hurry here. A good saké to relax with. A bit on the sweet side, but light and airy too. A crisper finish than one might imagine based on the kuchiatari, the initial taste sensation when a saké hits your palate. Goes well chilled, with neutral side dishes, and decent conversation.

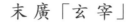

Suehiro
"Gensai" • *daiginjō*
Fukushima Prefecture

Nihonshu-do:	+4	Acidity:	1.3
Alcohol:	17.5%	Rice:	Yamada-Nishiki
Semaibuai:	35%	Yeast:	Proprietary

Gensai is the most attention-grabbing saké from this kura. It has a nice, high daiginjō nose that doesn't evaporate too quickly. The initial burst of flavor is full of autumn fruit, but this quickly melts into your tongue, and the flavor mellows and smoothens even more as it works its way almost deliberately toward your throat.

OTHER OFFERINGS: Suehiro saké is generally soft, delicate, and very easy to drink. There is a relatively wide variety of styles and tastes available.

大 和 川

Yamatogawa
Junmaishu
Fukushima Prefecture

Nihonshu-do:	+3	Acidity:	1.6
Alcohol:	15.3%	Rice:	Hanabuyuki
Semaibuai:	55%	Yeast:	Number 901

A rich and autumn-like nose, full of a blend of fruit and supported by a buttery or caramel-like essence. The flavors are well rounded, and seem fullest in the center of your tongue. A somewhat high acid presence gets your attention at first sip, and gives the saké a nice clean ending.

OTHER OFFERINGS: Yamatogawa makes a funky brew called Kasumochi that is brewed with more kōji than usual. A genshu with an alcohol content of almost 18%, it is quite sweet (nihonshu-do of –2) and has a honey-like nose and underlying flavor. Worth a try for sure.

清泉

Kiyoizumi

Tokubetsu junmaishu
Niigata Prefecture

Nihonshu-do:	+2	Acidity:	1.4
Alcohol:	15.3%	Rice:	Gohyakumangoku
Semaibuai:	55%	Yeast:	Number 10

Kiyoizumi is a saké that is both rich and subtle at the same time. It has quite a bit of flavor to it, but it all seems to lurk in the background of a well-balanced softness. The flavor and nose are both ricelike, with few of the esters that contribute to fruitiness. The fragrance seems to stay with you long after the sip is finished. It is not nearly as dry as most of the saké from this region, and gives you much more to pay attention to as well.

The *manga* (cartoon) series and television drama *Natsuko no Saké* was based on this kura, where a rice called Kame no Ō was revived, and a fine daiginjōshu made from it.

OTHER OFFERINGS: Kame no Ō, a daiginjōshu made from the rice of the same name, mentioned above, is the best-known saké from this kura.

Kubota

"Sen-ju" • *tokubetsu honjōzō*
Niigata Prefecture

Nihonshu-do:	+6	Acidity:	1.3
Alcohol:	15.3%	Rice:	Gohyakumangoku
Semaibuai:	57%	Yeast:	Number 9

Niigata saké tends to lend itself to generalizations, most of which are fortunately positive. The regional style is what is known as tanrei karakuchi, or light and dry. Kubota fits this description well. It is extremely clean, almost airy, and there is hardly any tail; the taste disappears quickly from your mouth and throat. It's dry and smooth from start to finish. Most definitely better when served cool or chilled.

Kubota is not so easy to find in retail stores, as it generally disappears from the shelves as quickly as the finish disappears from your palate. Many saké pubs carry this brew, and provide an excellent chance for sampling.

OTHER OFFERINGS: Kubota makes several sakés, including Hyaku-ju, Sen-ju, Man-ju, and Heki-ju, in increasing order of quality and price.

八 海 山

Hakkaisan
Junmai ginjōshu
Niigata Prefecture

Nihonshu-do:	+5	Acidity:	1.3
Alcohol:	15.5%	Rice:	Yamada-Nishiki
			Miyama-Nishiki
Semaibuai:	50%	Yeast:	Number 10

The nose is fairly subdued but not altogether forgotten in this saké. When you find the fragrance, it is clean and crisp. The flavor is a bit sharper than would be expected from the fragrance alone. There is a relatively bold acidity to the flavor, typical of a junmaishu but not so typical of the style of the region, perhaps.

OTHER OFFERINGS: Hakkaisan makes a very crisp and clean daiginjō with a nice nose and a softer flavor.

〆 張 鶴 「純」

Shimeharizuru
"Jun" • *junmai ginjōshu*
Niigata Prefecture

Nihonshu-do:	+3	Acidity:	1.4
Alcohol:	15.7%	Rice:	Gohyakumangoku
Semaibuai:	53%	Yeast:	Number 10

Shimeharizuru is another relatively famous saké from Niigata Prefecture. In general, the flavor is perhaps a bit smoother and softer than most Niigata saké, a distinction it shares with Kiyoizumi. This particular saké is clean, with a good acidity in the flavor that contrasts quite nicely with a gentle and inviting nose.

OTHER OFFERINGS: Shimeharizuru also has several more expensive and more refined saké offerings that are definitely worth a try if you should stumble upon them with cash in hand.

Kaganoi
Junmai ginjōshu
Niigata Prefecture

Nihonshu-do:	+5	Acidity:	1.5
Alcohol:	15 – 16%	Rice:	Gohyakumangoku
Semaibuai:	55%	Yeast:	Number 9

Brewing at this kura is done with water rising up from a well around which the brewery has been built. Kaganoi is clean and dry, but has more character and fullness than most typical saké from Niigata Prefecture, with a fragrant, flowery nose. A decently high but not obnoxious acid presence provides some personality. A nice ricelike essence throughout. Originally brewed for a feudal lord in neighboring Ishikawa Prefecture; hence the reference to the old name for that region (Kaga) in the meigara.

真澄

Masumi
Junmaishu
Nagano Prefecture

Nihonshu-do:	+3	Acidity:	1.9
Alcohol:	15 – 16%	Rice:	Miyama-Nishiki
Semaibuai:	60%	Yeast:	Number 9

Both a junmaishu and a honjōzō version of this saké are widely available. The former is better when served slightly chilled, while the latter is best for those who prefer warmed saké.

Masumi is just slightly on the dry side, and the taste spreads across your tongue quickly. It is a fairly heavy saké, in a good way, but with a very distinctive finish. The nose is faint but present, with just a slight acidity to it and not much sweetness. It manages to be the kind of saké that almost everyone likes, yet still maintains some uniqueness.

OTHER OFFERINGS: This kura also makes several daiginjō that are just as solid for their class, light and fragrant, gently flowery and fruity. Most notable is one called Yumedono.

七 笑

Nanawarai
Tokubetsu junmaishu
Nagano Prefecture

Nihonshu-do:	+1	Acidity:	1.5
Alcohol:	15.5%	Rice:	Miyama-Nishiki
Semaibuai:	60%	Yeast:	Number 1001

Nanawarai garnered a lot of attention when the ginjōshu fad began, with its reputation for distinction and consistency. A nice, comparatively heavy, full, and solid junmaishu. The acidity in the flavor seems to rise out of an enveloping softness to grab your attention. It rides a fine line between dry and sweet. A soft nose that doesn't run away on you, gently sweet and more flowery than fruity.

夜 明 け 前 「生 一 本」

Yoakemae

"Ki-ippon" • *junmaishu*
Nagano Prefecture

Nihonshu-do:	+1	Acidity:	1.5
Alcohol:	16 – 17%	Rice:	Miyama-Nishiki
Semaibuai:	50%	Yeast:	Alps yeast, Number 9 Number 10

A wonderfully prominent fragrance that leaps out at you, but evades all but the most dedicated attempts to nail it down. A plethora of fruit essences are hidden in this saké. The flavor is quite lively, with many facets vying for your attention. Fairly heavy and dense, and immensely satisfying; filling, solid, and memorable.

OTHER OFFERINGS: Ginkan-Shikomi ginjōshu is a slightly drier, lighter and more fragrant version of the above saké.

Reijin

Junmai ginjōshu
Nagano Prefecture

Nihonshu-do:	+5	Acidity:	1.5
Alcohol:	15 – 16%	Rice:	Miyama-Nishiki
Semaibuai:	60%	Yeast:	Alps yeast

Reijin is slightly dry, but its flavor still manages to keep a nice roundness. It enters your palate like a gift that unwraps itself halfway across your tongue. The nose is somewhat subdued, a bit shy, but seems to hang around in your mouth for a bit after the saké has gone down your throat. Overall, this saké has a soft sensation.

OTHER OFFERINGS: Reijin makes a somewhat more expressive daiginjō called Nozomi, and offers various koshu (aged saké) as well.

Ryūjin
"Ōze no Yukidoke" • *junmaishu*
Gunma Prefecture

Nihonshu-do:	+2	Acidity:	1.3
Alcohol:	15.5%	Rice:	Wakamizu
Semaibuai:	55%	Yeast:	Number 101

This is a fun saké that gives you a lot to pay attention to, and seems to change and present a different facet with each sip. The nose is fruity but light, without too much of a rice presence. Quite fresh and relatively unique, with lots of staying power.

The flavor seems to be sweet soon after it hits your tongue, but then all of a sudden becomes dry, finishing in a relatively shibui (astringent-tart) way. Most interesting at room temperature or slightly cooler.

OTHER OFFERINGS: Ōze no Yukidoke also comes in a honjōzō version that is a bit lighter, and may be more suited to warming.

四季桜

Shikizakura
"Hatsuhana" • *honjōzō*
Tochigi Prefecture

Nihonshu-do:	+2	Acidity:	1.3
Alcohol:	16.2	Rice:	Miyama-Nishiki
Semaibuai:	63%	Yeast:	Number 10

Hatsuhana is the flagship saké of Shikizakura. It has a fairly lively and thoroughly enjoyable nose, with fruity overtones. The flavor is smooth and constant throughout, ever so slightly on the softly sweet side. A soft and fading finish tops it off.

OTHER OFFERINGS: Shikizakura makes a very famous and sought-after daiginjō called Hijiri that is extremely difficult to get. There is also a popular junmai ginjōshu called Kaō.

東 力 士

Azuma Rikishi
Junmaishu
Tochigi Prefecture

Nihonshu-do:	±0	Acidity:	1.5
Alcohol:	15.4%	Rice:	Miyama-Nishiki
Semaibuai:	60%	Yeast:	Proprietary

This is one of those saké that reminds you that the beverage is made from rice, lest we forget. A nice, full flavor, that's quite rich, and filling in a way that is hard to describe for a comparatively light beverage like nihonshu. Characteristically sweeter than average saké. There is a subtle cocoa-like undercurrent, which contrasts well with the relatively crisp finish. The nose has the same quality of fullness found in the flavor.

渡 舟

Wataribune
Junmai daiginjōshu
Ibaraki Prefecture

Nihonshu-do:	+3	Acidity:	1.4
Alcohol:	16.5%	Rice:	Wataribune
Semaibuai:	35%	Yeast:	Number 9

Strains of sakamai, or rice used in making saké, change internally over time so that eventually they are no longer as suitable for making saké as they once were. Such rice strains can occasionally be revived if they have not been used for some time, however. Wataribune is a saké made with one such revived sakamai of the same name.

The flavor is rich and full, neither too dry nor too sweet. There is a light tangerine fruitiness to the fragrance that seems to be at once independent and connected to everything else. This saké seems to become significantly better with a bit of decanting.

OTHER OFFERINGS: There is also a ginjōshu version of Wataribune, and non-junmaishu versions as well. Fuchū Homare is the main saké of this kura.

Hitori Musume
"Sayaka" • *ginjōshu*
Ibaraki Prefecture

Nihonshu-do:	+6	Acidity:	1.5
Alcohol:	15.5%	Rice:	Miyama-Nishiki
Semaibuai:	55%	Yeast:	Number 9

Sayaka is an easy-to-spot bottle. It is available in many large stores stocking jizaké, and the word Sayaka is written in large hiragana characters across the label.

The flavor is bold and dry, with a relatively high acidity as well. It is sharp and clean, yet balanced. The most prominent overall quality of the flavor is the shibumi, usually translated as "astringency" in English. Each sip is an eye-opener. There are very few off-flavors, and the fragrance is faint but clean and well connected to the rest of the saké.

Sayaka is great at room temperature or thereabout. Etiher too much chilling or excessive heating will rob this saké of its distinction.

武勇「しぼりたて」

Buyū
"Shiboritate" • *junmaishu*
Ibaraki Prefecture

Nihonshu-do:	+2	Acidity:	1.3
Alcohol:	15 – 16%	Rice:	Gohyakumangoku
Semaibuai:	55%	Yeast:	Number 9

This version of Buyū is unpasteurized and unfiltered. It is only available in the spring and early summer. Fresh and lively, it has a slightly rough edge to it that is deliberate and defining. The nose is fairly well pronounced, slightly sweeter than the taste of the saké would lead you to believe. The flavor is somewhat dry, with a touch of some citrus fruit and a slight stabilizing bitterness underneath it all.

The flavor components all blend together to give it an overall gentleness. Heating Buyū would not be the best choice; serve it slightly chilled.

筑 波

Tsukuba
Daiginjō
Ibaraki Prefecture

Nihonshu-do:	+4	Acidity:	1.3
Alcohol:	17.5%	Rice:	Akaiwa Ōmachi
Semaibuai:	39%	Yeast:	Number 9

A truly wonderfully balanced saké with a light but definitive and seductive fragrance to it. The flavor spreads quickly, but not instantaneously, into and across your mouth. The flavor is textured, and a pleasant grainy flavor profile tickles your tongue for a second or two, then disappears just the way it appeared — quickly but not instantaneously. Probably better when served cool or even well-chilled, but warming would deprive this brew of its ability to express itself.

OTHER OFFERINGS: Tsukuba comes in various other styles, including junmaishu, namazaké, as well as several manifestations of ginjōshu.

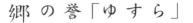

Sato-no-Homare
"Yusura" • *nama junmai ginjōshu*
Ibaraki Prefecture

Nihonshu-do:	+2	Acidity:	Not available
Alcohol:	16%	Rice:	Yamada-Nishiki
Semaibuai:	Information not available	Yeast:	Proprietary

This kura has the distinction of holding the oldest written records of saké making, going back to 1141. The present president is the fifty-fourth in line. This saké is smooth and very drinkable; it hits the palate with a light fruitiness and a nice crisp feel. Like a typical namazaké, it spreads around your tongue with great liveliness. The fragrance is stable and not too pronounced, fruity in a gentle and mellow way. The flavor and smell seem to linger and almost return after the saké has passed down your throat.

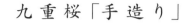

Kokonoe-zakura
"Tezukui" • *junmaishu*
Saitama Prefecture

Nihonshu-do:	+2	Acidity:	1.4
Alcohol:	15.4%	Rice:	Wakamizu
Semaibuai:	60%	Yeast:	Number 901

Extremely crisp, full of lively flavors, and quite distinctive, the nose is neither too overpowering nor too hard to find; it is clean and effervescently fruity. This saké is a bit softer and more coy than the average junmaishu, which gives it a special appeal.

OTHER OFFERINGS: Kokonoe-zakura makes several excellent ginjōshu with bold but extremely clean and balanced apple-like fruitiness to them. Not to be missed.

125

鏡 山

Kagamiyama
Ginjōshu
Saitama Prefecture

Nihonshu-do:	+3	Acidity:	1.2
Alcohol:	16.5%	Rice:	Yamada-Nishiki
Semaibuai:	40 – 50%	Yeast:	Number 9

A mellow nose with a light fruitiness that is quite distinctive. This fragrance remains with you well into the sip, and seems to be even more pronounced just before you swallow. Quite unique. The flavor is well-rounded, and a collage of tastes spreads quickly and decisively over your palate. The balance is so fine that it could all too easily be taken for granted.

神亀「ひこ孫」

Shinkame
"Hikomago" • *junmai ginjōshu*
Saitama Prefecture

Nihonshu-do:	+4	Acidity:	1.4
Alcohol:	15.4%	Rice:	Yamada-Nishiki,
			Miyama-Nishiki
Semaibuai:	50%	Yeast:	Number 7 or
			Number 9

Hikomago is much more distinctive than the statistics would indicate. It's got a mouth-puckering impact that is eye-opening, without going too far. This flavor profile consists of more than just acidity, though; it's a fascinating combination of various elements. Great with tempura or other dishes which might be slightly oily. Perhaps one of the best saké available for warming, it really comes into its own when served as o-kan.

OTHER OFFERINGS: A daiginjō version of Hikomago is also available, and Shinkame makes an excellent nigorizaké as well.

澤乃井

Sawanoi
Junmai ginjōshu
Tokyo

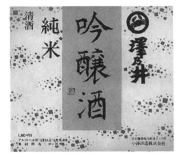

Nihonshu-do:	+3	Acidity:	1.5
Alcohol:	15.5%	Rice:	Gohyakumangoku
Semaibuai:	60%	Yeast:	Number 9

The kuchiatari, or impression given upon the first drink, for this saké is dry and crisp, but soon after the flavor softens and spreads out. Generally clean and dry throughout, it has a fairly quickly evaporating tail with a nice sharp acidic touch to it. The nose is subdued but pleasant, gentle, and flowery. This is not a bad choice for warming, as it will retain its smoothness, but it is perhaps better when served chilled. At room temperature, its distinction goes into hiding.

Tsukimaru
Junmaishu
Tokyo

Nihonshu-do:	+2	Acidity:	1.4
Alcohol:	15.5%	Rice:	Miyama-Nishiki
Semaibuai:	60%	Yeast:	Japan Saké Brewers' Association strain

A well-rounded and well-balanced saké, lively and eye-opening. A good acidic presence and a touch of sweetness cooperate to present a clean and vibrant flavor profile. A fairly prominent fragrance ties it all together.

OTHER OFFERINGS: Tsukimaru has been making some excellent ginjōshu over the past few years, suddenly appearing on the prize-winning scene of late. At least in the Tokyo area, their various ginjōshu offerings are not hard to find, and are well worth the minimal effort it takes to track them down.

岩 の 井

Iwanoi
Daiginjōshu
Chiba Prefecture

Nihonshu-do:	+4	Acidity:	1.2
Alcohol:	16.5%	Rice:	Yamada-Nishiki
Semaibuai:	50%	Yeast:	Number 9

The fragrance of this saké is sweet and fruity, but not in an exaggerated way. The flavor is more dry than sweet, but full of other qualities as well. An outstanding example of how good ginjōshu can get. Uniquely appealing. Serve just slightly chilled.

OTHER OFFERINGS: Iwanoi also makes an *ichidan-shikomi yamahai-shikomi,* which means all the rice was added at once, instead of in three stages. It is fairly smooth, with flavor components that are quite a bit different from the average saké.

天青 「千峰天青」

Tensei
"Senpō" • junmai ginjōshu
Kanagawa Prefecture

Nihonshu-do:	+2	Acidity:	1.2
Alcohol:	15%	Rice:	Yamada-Nishiki
Seimaibuai:	50%	Yeast:	Proprietary

A mild aroma slightly reminiscent of grapes, but with solid ricelike underpinnings, leads invitingly to a straightforward, well-constructed flavor profile. Slightly full, only just on the rich side, and balanced. Ever so slightly nutty and herbal in the recesses of the flavor.

The brand name Tensei has only been around since 2001. (Prior to 2001, the brewery used other brand names.) It was just about then that a new, young tōji took the reins and began to focus on making his own style of great saké. So far, so good.

開 運

Kaiun
Junmai ginjōshu
Shizuoka Prefecture

Nihonshu-do:	+5	Acidity:	1.5
Alcohol:	16.5%	Rice:	Gohyakumangoku, Yamada-Nishiki
Semaibuai:	55%	Yeast:	Shizuoka Kōbo

A wonderfully balanced ginjōshu that is not overbearing in any one way. It comes to your palate softly, and different flavor elements appear as it moves across your tongue. Sometimes sweet, sometimes tangy, but always gentle and balanced. The fragrance is calm and quiet, hinting at flowers in bloom.

OTHER OFFERINGS: Kaiun very consistently makes excellent saké on all levels. The more you taste, the more you appreciate. Their daiginjō saké are distinctive, usually straying slightly and tastefully from the mainstream.

若竹鬼ころし

Wakatake Onikoroshi
(Onikoroshi Wakatake)
Honjōzō
Shizuoka Prefecture

Nihonshu-do:	+9	Acidity:	1.3
Alcohol:	17.5%	Rice:	Gohyakumangoku, Ōgonbare
Semaibuai:	60%	Yeast:	New Number 5

This small brewery makes what is perhaps the most famous saké in Japan, called Onikoroshi, or Demon Killer. This term was previously used to refer to a saké that was so bad it could kill a demon, but a kura in Gifu Prefecture had the courage to reverse the phrase's meaning. They deliberately called their saké Onikoroshi, implying that it was so good it could kill a demon. The name stuck, and there are many Onikoroshi saké today, most dry and strong, but few as good as this one.

OTHER OFFERINGS: Wakatake also makes a daiginjōshu called Onna Nakase, or Make the Ladies Cry. Clean, smooth, and explicit in its expression of flavor, it is a soft and full saké, with a very subdued fragrance.

磯 自 慢

Isojiman
Honjōzō
Shizuoka Prefecture

Nihonshu-do:	+6 – +8	Acidity:	1.1
Alcohol:	15 – 16%	Rice:	Yamada-Nishiki
			Gohyakumangoku
Semaibuai:	55 – 60%	Yeast:	New 5

Isojiman's saké may be a bit hard to find outside of Shizuoka Prefecture, but it is worth the effort. The honjōzō has a bright, cheerful, fresh, and flowery nose; it's crisp but with not a lot of fruitiness. The flavor itself is dry, clear, and sharp. Very crisp. The flavor is strongest somewhere in the middle, between the time you first sip it and the time it moves down your throat. The acidity is low, and the kuchiatari is relatively soft. Dry finish with a very slight bitterness.

OTHER OFFERINGS: If you can find it, Isojiman's daiginjō is smooth and fragrant. They make nothing lower than honjōzō grade, and everything brewed here rings of quality and pride of workmanship.

明 眸

Meibō
Junmaishu
Aichi Prefecture

Nihonshu-do:	+1.5	Acidity:	1.4
Alcohol:	14.8%	Rice:	Gohyakumangoku, Wakamizu
Semaibuai:	58%	Yeast:	Number 9

Fairly soft at first, the flavor of this saké opens up to reveal some interesting aspects. Perhaps best when just slightly under room temperature, a light sweetness rides on top of some slight fruit flavors and a touch of acidity. There is a very settled nuance to the flavor, and it stays on your tongue with no intention of moving until it is ready, eventually fading in a pleasing manner.

Tairin
Junmai ginjōshu
Gifu Prefecture

Nihonshu-do:	+1	Acidity:	1.2
Alcohol:	15.6%	Rice:	Yamada-Nishiki
Semaibuai:	50%	Yeast:	Number 9

The fragrance for this saké is prominent, indicative of light and acidic fruit such as cantaloupe, and refuses to fade. The flavor seems most prominent in the back of your palate and on your throat, and almost sneaks in before you realize it. Neither dry nor sweet, a flavor that defies description. It's worth the effort to find this saké.

OTHER OFFERINGS: Tairin makes another ginjōshu called Mizore-zake, which is a bit lighter and fresher in style.

Nagaragawa
Junmaishu
Gifu Prefecture

Nihonshu-do:	+6	Acidity:	1.8
Alcohol:	15 – 16%	Rice:	Hidahomare
Semaibuai:	66%	Yeast:	Number 7

This small kura has about twenty stereo speakers that play music and natural sounds around the fermenting tanks twenty-four hours a day. Does it help? Try Nagaragawa and see.

There is a very light fruitiness to the nose that seems grapefruit-like, a sensation no doubt affected by the high acidity. The flavor spreads out well with a good amount of body, but is actually light overall. Fairly dry with a good exit, it goes well chilled or gently warmed.

Wakaebisu
"Maho" • *yamahai-shikomi junmai ginjōshu*
Mie Prefecture

Nihonshu-do:	+3	Acidity:	1.5
Alcohol:	16.2%	Rice:	Gohyakumangoku
Semaibuai:	53%	Yeast:	Number 9

Maho has a relatively high acid presence in its flavor, and a lot of body to support it. There is a very pleasant but hard-to-describe quality gently pervading the flavor and fragrance, that's almost nutty. Beyond this, it is quite clean, with very disjointed components in the flavor. Maho is a wonderful choice for warming, but is tasty when cooler as well.

Maho may be a bit harder to find than the average saké, but the bottle is easy to spot. It is wrapped in plain brown corrugated paper. The neck is tied with a natural-looking hemplike cord, and the label is at a forty-five-degree angle, as if it has been slapped on haphazardly.

OTHER OFFERINGS: Wakaebisu makes several other saké that all have their own appeal.

Biwa-no-chōju
Junmai ginjō
Shiga Prefecture

Nihonshu-do:	+4	Acidity:	1.7
Alcohol:	15.4%	Rice:	Tamazakae
Semaibuai:	50%	Yeast:	Number 10

Biwa-no-chōju is a small kura in a land of small kura. At last count, Shiga Prefecture had sixty-five kura, yet it is only fortieth on the list of prefectures in terms of the amount of saké it produces. Shiga Prefecture is also known as the home of a very old saké rice called Tamazakae, used in some Biwa-no-chōju.

The junmai ginjō is a lovely saké with a fairly high acidity. This is typical of most of the saké from this kura, if not from the region. Yet this aspect is balanced by the amami (sweetness) and nigami (bitterness) that hang around the background of the flavor. The fragrance is sweet and mildly fruity, more citrus than anything else, but it is far from overpowering.

OTHER OFFERINGS: Biwa-no-chōju also makes a truly outstanding namazaké called Kurabito and a thick and chewy nigorizaké that are admittedly hard to find, but worth the search.

秋 鹿 「摂 州 能 勢」

Akishika
"Sesshū Nōse" • *tokubetsu junmaishu*
Osaka Prefecture

Nihonshu-do:	+2	Acidity:	1.5
Alcohol:	15 – 16%	Rice:	Tamazakae,
			Yamada-Nishiki
Semaibuai:	60%	Yeast:	Number 1001

This saké has a unique nose, fruity, acidic, and milky all at once. It hits your palate with a full and soft kuchiatari (first impression), and the flavor continues to be full throughout. Overall, the flavor is soft, but with an acidic touch around the edges. It has a certain appeal when slightly warmed.

あ ま の 酒 「吉 祥」

Amanozake
"Kishō" • *ginjōshu*
Osaka Prefecture

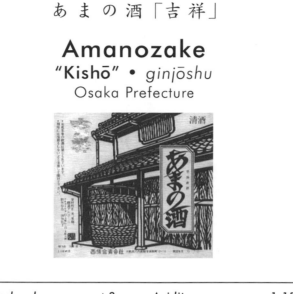

Nihonshu-do:	+3	Acidity:	1.15
Alcohol:	15.7%	Rice:	Yamada-Nishiki, Hattan-Nishiki
Semaibuai:	49%	Yeast:	Number 901

Unfortunately, this saké is hard to find outside of Osaka. This brew has a bright, vibrant, fruity nose, with lots of esters apparent. The flavor spreads quickly across your tongue, and settles in for a second. It's gone as quickly as it arrived, disappearing from both the palate and the throat at the same time. Quite enjoyable. Quite different at room temperature versus chilled.

利 休 梅

Rikyūbai
Junmai ginjō
Osaka Prefecture

Nihonshu-do:	+4	Acidity:	1.8
Alcohol:	15 – 16%	Rice:	Yamada-Nishiki
Seimaibuai:	55%	Yeast:	Number 9

Overall a very balanced saké, neither overtly dry nor overtly sweet, and somewhat full in flavor. A slightly weighty presence on the palate is wonderfully bolstered by an excellent defining acidity. The fragrance, too, strikes a great balance with the flavor in its intensity and duration.

OTHER OFFERINGS: This brewery also makes a line of saké called "Mukune" — a reference to an ancient village — that can be loosely translated as "the root of innocence." The Mukune series is brewed with locally grown rice.

Umenoyado
Junmai ginjōshu
Nara Prefecture

Nihonshu-do:	+5	Acidity:	1.4
Alcohol:	16.2%	Rice:	Yamada-Nishiki, Kita-Nishiki
Semaibuai:	50%	Yeast:	Number 9

This saké has richness and a well-rounded flavor in good balance. It is neither too sweet nor too dry; rather, the overriding quality is of fullness on the palate. The fragrance is quite complete; it seems to have a bit of everything in just the right measure. A slight rice fragrance is wrapped in ever-so-slight fruity scents. The flavor sensation seems to stay strong from the beginning to the end, but then evaporates quite quickly leaving you wondering where it went in such a hurry.

OTHER OFFERINGS: This small kura makes many fine saké of all classes. Their honjōzō is excellent warmed, its daiginjō are prize-winners, and their yamahai-shikomi is complex but extremely subtle. Don't miss their stuff.

山鶴

Yamatsuru
Junmai daiginjō
Nara Prefecture

Nihonshu-do:	+4	Acidity:	1.4
Alcohol:	16.8%	Rice:	Miyama-Nishiki
Semaibuai:	50%	Yeast:	Number 9

Here at this tiny kura the average semaibuai is 50%, and nothing is over 60%. All the brewer's alcohol used here is fermented from saké kasu (lees) as well. A very soft and seductive nose leads to a rich and full flavor that is clean and slightly dry overall. The flavor takes its time about moving across your palate, as opposed to exploding.

Shōtoku
Tokubetsu honjōzō
Kyoto

Nihonshu-do:	+1	Acidity:	1.4
Alcohol:	15 – 16%	Rice:	Gohyakumangoku,
			Nihonhomare
Semaibuai:	60%	Yeast:	Number 9

The overall sensation upon drinking this saké is one of softness, with a gently sweet flavor on top. This saké, typical of the Kyoto Fushimi style of saké, results from the wonderful water used in brewing. Lots of supporting flavor elements give Shōtoku a nice full-bodied texture, but none of these elements is overly prominent. A soft and almost buttery nose.

Tomiō
"Ginrei" • junmai daiginjō
Kyoto

Nihonshu-do:	+3	Acidity:	1.3
Alcohol:	15.8	Rice:	Gohyakumangoku, Akebono
Semaibuai:	45%	Yeast:	KK-9

This saké has a fragrance that's strongly indicative of sweeter fruits, and low on the acidity. The flavor spreads quite nicely across the palate, but at its own typically Kyoto-brewed saké pace. Light and fairly lively, this gentle and somewhat feminine saké never fails to satisfy, and it's all too easy to go through a bottle quickly. Generally better if served cool, but adventurous souls might try it warm.

小 鼓

Kotsuzumi
Junmaishu
Hyogo Prefecture

Nihonshu-do:	+6	Acidity:	1.4
Alcohol:	15.8%	Rice:	Hyogo Kita-Nishiki
Semaibuai:	60%	Yeast:	Number 10

Kotsuzumi differs just a bit from the saké that are typical for this region. There seems to be a faint touch of citrus in the nose, which is quiet and almost hidden. The flavor is not overly strong, and has a smooth, creamy, banana-like element to it, but you have to look for it. This and other flavor elements blend well together.

The flavor profile of this saké changes quite a bit when it is warmed or chilled. A good saké to educate your palate with.

富久錦「静香流麗」

Fukunishiki
"Seikaryūrei" • junmai ginjōshu
Hyogo Prefecture

Nihonshu-do:	+1	Acidity:	1.5
Alcohol:	15 – 16%	Rice:	Yamada-Nishiki,
			Gohyakumangoku
Semaibuai:	50%	Yeast:	Number 9

All of the saké made at this kura is junmaishu; no saké has any added brewer's alcohol. If nothing else, this means they are very good at what they do.

The nose of this particular saké is what you might expect from a solid junmaishu — slightly tart and acidic, with perhaps some grape-fruit involved, but no real ester fragrances like apples or bananas. This is a nice example of the junmaishu style.

A high-impact kuchiatari and a strong acidity make this saké ideal with food like tempura. Despite a fairly light body, the fukurami, or spreading sensation throughout one's mouth, is fast and thorough. Room temperature is recommended when serving this saké with food, but warming it gently may make it more suitable for drinking by itself.

Takinokoi
Junmai ginjōshu
Hyogo Prefecture

Nihonshu-do:	+2	Acidity:	1.6
Alcohol:	15%	Rice:	Yamada-Nishiki, Kōrei-Nishiki
Semaibuai:	60%	Yeast:	Number 10

A nice, quiet fragrance is a somewhat deceiving façade for the fairly full flavor that greets your palate with this saké. The flavor components are well blended and quite refined. The tail is a bit sweeter than the rest of the flavor profile might lead you to expect. Takinokoi has its respective charms at both slightly chilled and slightly warmed serving temperatures.

手取川「酒魂」

Tedorigawa
"Sakadamashii" • *ginjōshu*
Ishikawa Prefecture

Nihonshu-do:	+4 – +5	Acidity:	1.3 – 1.5
Alcohol:	15.5%	Rice:	Yamada-Nishiki
Semaibuai:	50%	Yeast:	Number 9

Tedorigawa is a crisp, clean, and light saké that draws your attention to it with every sip. The acidity seems to be just about perfect when compared to the rest of the flavor profile. As a rather light saké, this is a rather mean feat, yet somehow it is achieved.

The nose is light, with a touch of apples, and seems to last a long time. It is well defined, and seems as if it has been chosen with care to match the rest of the saké's qualities.

Tedorigawa is nice chilled, although some interesting components come out of hiding when it warms up to room temperature.

OTHER OFFERINGS: Tedorigawa makes a wonderful namazaké, available in the spring, although it may be somewhat hard to find.

菊 姫

Kikuhime
Yamahai-shikomi junmaishu
Ishikawa Prefecture

Nihonshu-do:	+1	Acidity:	2.2
Alcohol:	16.5%	Rice:	Yamada-Nishiki
Semaibuai:	65%	Yeast:	Number 7

Kikuhime's yamahai is a rich and flavorful brew, very solid and distinctive. It is extremely characteristic of the yamahai style, and, in a good way, tends to be on the rough side. The acidity is mouth-puckeringly high, as is often the case with yamahai, but it maintains its balance and has a noticeably quick finish.

It also has a pleasing amber color that matches its flavor. Its distinct taste is better at cooler temperatures or when warmed.

OTHER OFFERINGS: Kikuhime makes many excellent saké, all of which are distinctive and well defined. Rich, balanced, and fragrant, you can't go wrong with anything they brew.

萬歳楽「加賀の白山」

Manzairaku
"Kaga no Hakusan" • *daiginjō koshu*
Ishikawa Prefecture

Nihonshu-do:	+5	Acidity:	1.3
Alcohol:	16 – 17%	Rice:	Yamada-Nishiki
Semaibuai:	40%	Yeast:	Number 9

This koshu (aged saké) has been aged three years, and nothing was spared in its production. The highest grade of Yamada-Nishiki rice was used for brewing, and this was polished enough to keep Kaga no Hakusan smooth throughout the aging process. The flavor is light, crisp, and airy, but well defined. The nose is fruity and balanced, without being overpowering in the least. The positive effects of aging are quite recognizable: all the flavors seem to get along with each other better than in most saké. If only people were sure to age this gracefully.

Kaga no Hakusan daiginjō koshu is not cheap, but is worth every yen.

OTHER OFFERINGS: Manzairaku makes several other fine saké, including a decent yamahai and a nonaged version of Hakusan that is significantly less expensive.

成 政 「純」

Narimasa
"Jun" • *junmaishu*
Toyama Prefecture

Nihonshu-do:	+3	Acidity:	1.4
Alcohol:	14.8%	Rice:	Gohyakumangoku
Semaibuai:	60%	Yeast:	Number 9

Narimasa comes from a fairly small kura with a fairly large reputation. Although they make several fine saké of various classes, their junmaishu, known simply as Jun, is stable and dependable. The flavor is dry, yet quite full, with a discernible rice flavor. It is smooth and soft, and the nose hangs around until the saké gets across your throat. It's easy to drink a lot of this one, so be careful.

OTHER OFFERINGS: Narimasa makes a honjōzō that is a bit lighter and perhaps sweeter than the junmaishu. They also make several light but flavorful ginjōshu that have a very fast and clean kire, or finish.

満寿泉

Masuizumi
Ginjōshu
Toyama Prefecture

Nihonshu-do:	+5	Acidity:	1.4
Alcohol:	15.8%	Rice:	Yamada-Nishiki,
			Hattan-Nishiki,
			Gohyakumangoku
Semaibuai:	58%	Yeast:	Number 9

A light and sweet, fruity nose that takes some sniffing to find. The flavor is clean and quite narrow, free from too many distracting elements that would only clutter it. In general, this saké is a bit on the dry side, with some sweeter elements around the edges. The flavor disappears fairly quickly, leaving you eager for another sip. Better cool than at room temperature.

銀盤「播州50」

Ginban
"Banshū 50" • *junmai ginjōshu*
Toyama Prefecture

Nihonshu-do:	+4	Acidity:	1.3
Alcohol:	15%	Rice:	Yamada-Nishiki
Semaibuai:	50%	Yeast:	Number 9

The first kanji character used in writing Banshū refers to Harima, the old name for the region in Hyogo Prefecture where the rice used in this saké, Yamada-Nishiki, is grown. The 50 refers to the semaibuai. The nose is nice and gentle, soft and a touch nutty. The flavor is immensely satisfying in an indescribable way. This saké is very tasty and very easy to drink. A different character presents itself at each serving temperature. The nose is best slightly chilled, but this is a satisfying and filling saké when warmed also.

立山「吟麗立山」

Tateyama
"Ginrei Tateyama" • *ginjōshu*
Toyama Prefecture

Nihonshu-do:	+4.5 – 5.5	Acidity:	1.5
Alcohol:	15.5%	Rice:	Yamada-Nishiki
Semaibuai:	58%	Yeast:	Number 9

This brewery has two brewing locations and two tōji, who happen to be father and son. Their saké is gentle and mature. It avoids frivolous fruity essences, presenting instead a settled and mellow ricelike fragrance and flavor profile. There is a certain richness to this saké that is hard to describe. No single flavor is overpowering, and they all blend well into a conservative but enjoyable drink.

Kokuryū
Junmai ginjōshu
Fukui Prefecture

Nihonshu-do:	+3	Acidity:	1.4
Alcohol:	15.5%	Rice:	Gohyakumangoku
Semaibuai:	55%	Yeast:	Proprietary

Kokuryū seems to be just slightly different each time you taste it. It's quite complex. The nose alone has several kinds of fruit popping up at different times, including apples, melons, and persimmons, yet this fruitiness is by no means overpowering. The flavor is just a bit on the dry side, but heads toward neutral as it warms up to room temperature.

Kokuryū is fairly light, and the acidity is low as well. "Slender" seems to be a fitting description, implying that there is not much excess baggage. Even so, different aspects of its flavor seem to appear each time it is tasted.

OTHER OFFERINGS: There is a daiginjōshu version called Shizuku that is quite prized in the region that this saké comes from, and therefore rarely makes it out of Fukui Prefecture.

157

花 垣

Hanagaki
Junmai ginjōshu
Fukui Prefecture

Nihonshu-do:	+3	Acidity:	1.6
Alcohol:	15 – 16%	Rice:	Gohyakumangoku
Semaibuai:	50%	Yeast:	Number 9

A light and vibrant nose with a healthy amount of esters gives this saké a strong fruit sensation. This is a light and refreshing saké without a lot of clutter in its flavor. It's fairly clean and straightforward, slightly dry, and very fresh-tasting. The flavor is fairly constant from the time you sip it until the last drop disappears down your throat.

賀茂泉「本仕込」

Kamoizumi
"Hon-Shikomi" • *junmai ginjōshu*
Hiroshima Prefecture

Nihonshu-do:	+1.5	Acidity:	1.8%
Alcohol:	15.8	Rice:	Hattan-Nishiki
Semaibuai:	60%	Yeast:	Number 9

Basically a dry saké with a nice clean finish, Kamoizumi has several other distinguishing characteristics. The bitterness (nigami) and astringency-tartness-pucker flavor (shibumi) are a bit higher than average, yet they are balanced and not at all out of place within the overall range of flavors. The nose is somewhat citric, and it changes slightly to include other fruit essences as you sniff.

Although Kamoizumi is quite good chilled, it seems to really come into its own when it warms up a bit, near room temperature. Don't be afraid to warm it even further; it makes an excellent choice for kan-zaké (warmed saké).

OTHER OFFERINGS: Kamoizumi makes several ginjōshu-class saké at slightly different prices. There is also a fine daiginjō called Kotobuki.

富久長

Fukuchō
Junmaishu
Hiroshima Prefecture

Nihonshu-do:	+4	Acidity:	1.4
Alcohol:	15.9%	Rice:	Hattan-Nishiki
Semaibuai:	60%	Yeast:	Number 9

The water used in brewing this saké is extremely soft. This helps create a saké that spreads quickly across your palate and melts on your tongue just as quickly. Its mellow flavor profile seems to have some citrus fruit running beneath everything else. Serving Fukuchō gently warmed seems to do it justice.

OTHER OFFERINGS: Fukuchō's daiginjō is a complex and layered brew — balanced and flavorful. A good example of daiginjō at its best.

Kinsen
"Saké Hyaku Yaku no Chō"
nama junmai ginjōshu
Hiroshima Prefecture

Nihonshu-do:	+2	Acidity:	1.2
Alcohol:	15-16%	Rice:	Hattan-Nishiki
Semaibuai:	50%	Yeast:	KA-1

The name of this saké means something like: saké is the best of all medicine. Its very light and clean flavor is preceded by a gentle but inviting nose that's slightly sweet but not in a fruity way. Generally light, it's quickly absorbed by your palate. There is a hidden quality here that is shared by all Kinsen saké. Hard to find but worth the search.

Hanahato
"Ginjō-zukuri" • *junmaishu*
Hiroshima Prefecture

Nihonshu-do:	+2.5	*Acidity:*	1.5
Alcohol:	16.5%	*Rice:*	Hattan
Semaibuai:	50%	*Yeast:*	Kumamoto Yeast

A very clean flavor and not a lot of body allow this saké to go down smoothly and quickly. It tastes more acidic than its numbers would indicate, and this can get in the way at higher temperatures. Overchilling should also be avoided. Served slightly cool, it goes well with tempura.

酒一筋「☆☆☆」

Saké Hitosuji
"☆☆☆" • *junmai ginjōshu*
Okayama Prefecture

Nihonshu-do:	+3	Acidity:	1.6
Alcohol:	15 – 16%	Rice:	Akaiwa Ōmachi
Semaibuai	52%	Yeast:	TS Number 9

Saké Hitosuji is made from a very old, local rice whose special qualities give it a boldness that causes the individual flavor components to assert themselves rather than blend together. This imparts a spicy sensation to the overall taste profile.

The fragrance is slightly spicy and fruity, and not so much strong as consistent. The flavor is fairly dry, but inspired. The individual flavors compete with each other, then disappear together quickly in a wonderful *kire,* or exit, from your palate. Good chilled, but excellent when gently warmed.

OTHER OFFERINGS: Saké Hitosuji also makes a saké that goes by the name "☆☆", as well as a wonderful daiginjō. Both are enjoyable served warm as well as chilled.

歓 の 泉

Yorokobi no Izumi
Nama junmai ginjōshu
Okayama Prefecture

Nihonshu-do:	+4	Acidity:	1.4
Alcohol:	17 – 18%	Rice:	Ōmachi
Semaibuai:	50%	Yeast:	Number 9

A nice and inviting nose draws you into a rich but never overpowering flavor with this saké. The various components of the flavor profile tend to be individually discernible if you look for them. This saké seems to be best when served a bit on the chilly side, since all the flavors tighten up and blend a bit more completely. This kura isn't huge, so it can be a bit difficult to find their saké.

Gozenshu
"Mimasaka" • *junmaishu*
Okayama Prefecture

Nihonshu-do:	+3	Acidity:	1.6
Alcohol:	15.5%	Rice: Ōmachi, Nihonbare	
Semaibuai:	60%	Yeast:	Number 9

A faint but slightly spicy nose, with just a hint of cinnamon in it marks this saké. The flavor has a strong acidity to it, but rather than being distracting it seems to tie together all the other flavor components. It spreads well across your mouth and fades cleanly.

OTHER OFFERINGS: Gozenshu makes an expensive but well-crafted and complex daiginjō called Hō-ō, that is designed to be served warm, rare for something four times the price of the average saké.

諏 訪 泉 「鵬」

Suwaizumi
"Ōtori" • *daiginjoshu*
Tottori Prefecture

Nihonshu-do:	±0	Acidity:	1.3
Alcohol:	16.5%	Rice:	Yamada-Nishiki
Semaibuai:	40%	Yeast:	Number 9

This saké does a wonderful job of resisting description in words. Ōtori has a subdued but slightly flowery fragrance that draws you into the saké itself. The flavor is soft, neither dry nor sweet, and melts well on your tongue. There is an interesting richness, subtle and almost hidden, that is almost buttery in nature. It takes an instant or so, but the flavor rises up after a soft kuchiatari, and then dies out just as it crosses your throat.

OTHER OFFERINGS: The regular saké from this kura is called Suwaizumi, and there are several good types of saké available under this name. All are generally soft and slightly sweet.

君司

Kimitsukasa
Junmai ginjōshu
Tottori Prefecture

Nihonshu-do:	+3	Acidity:	1.4
Alcohol:	15.5%	Rice:	Tamazakae
Semaibuai:	50%	Yeast:	Number 9

Made from a very old saké-brewing rice in use today, this saké has the typical dense and "fat" qualities found in a junmaishu. But there are also a lot of hidden flavor components dancing around in the background that you can completely miss if you are not looking for them.

OTHER OFFERINGS: A delicious and very reasonably priced daiginjō called Kyoku-gin is also available from the Kimitsukasa brewery.

Rihaku
Junmai ginjōshu
Shimane Prefecture

Nihonshu-do:	+4	Acidity:	1.6
Alcohol:	15 – 16%	Rice:	Yamada-Nishiki
Semaibuai:	55%	Yeast:	Number 9

Several Shimane Prefecture saké, Rihaku included, share a particular distinction that is quite a refreshing change from more popular and standard saké. This saké has a definite yet very subtle tartness that makes it unique. Tartness may not sound like a quality associated with decent nihonshu, but it definitely works in this saké. The relatively high acidity contributes to both the tartness and a flavor that is drier than the nihonshu-do would suggest. A wonderful saké to enjoy with food in general.

The fragrance is decisive but not overpowering, and is remarkably indicative of the flavor to come. There is a citrus-like fruitiness to it that lends a clean and sharp quality to the saké's overall profile.

OTHER OFFERINGS: Rihaku makes several grades of saké, all of which share a wonder thread of distinction.

Toyo no Aki
Tokubetsu junmaishu
Shimane Prefecture

Nihonshu-do:	±0	Acidity:	1.5
Alcohol:	15.5%	Rice:	Kairyō Ōmachi,
			Hyogo Kita-Nishiki
Semaibuai:	58%	Yeast:	Number 9

Some saké has an unforgettable distinction, often an extremely deli-cate one. Toyo no Aki is one such saké. It is neither dry nor sweet. In fact it seems to ride the razor-thin line between these two extremes. The flavor of rice is apparent, rather than a fruity fragrance.

Within a softness is found a round and full balance of flavors that play off of one another very well. Both in the fragrance and in the fla-vor are hints of some heavier, nuttier flavors, as well as some lighter fruitier facets. This saké is wonderful at different temperatures, each of which brings out a different facet of the saké's character. Room temperature seems to give rise to the best results.

月山

Gassan
Junmai ginjōshu
Shimane Prefecture

Nihonshu-do:	+4.5	Acidity:	1.5
Alcohol:	15.8	Rice:	Yamada-Nishiki,
			Kairyō Ōmachi
Semaibuai:	55%	Yeast:	Number 9

Gassan is typical of a flavor commonly found in Shimane Prefecture saké; somewhat rich and full-bodied, with a fairly high acidity. This style is indicative of the Izumo Tōji Ryūha (brew masters' guild) in this region.

Gassan has a fruity sweetness that is supported by an underlying acidity. The kuchiatari is lively and bright, and the zesty quality of the saké remains with all of its balance until it is long past your throat. The nose is infused with a delicate scent of persimmons and a touch of acidity.

OTHER OFFERINGS: Gassan also makes a definitive daiginjō called Ōgi.

Asahi Tenyū
Junmai ginjōshu
Shimane Prefecture

Nihonshu-do:	+5	Acidity:	1.2
Alcohol:	15.3%	Rice:	Kairyō Ōmachi
Semaibuai:	55%	Yeast:	Number 9

This saké has a very interesting but subdued nose: soft, a touch buttery, with a smidgen of ripe plums, persimmons, and maybe figs. This fragrance works well and draws you into the saké's flavor.

The strange combination of fruit described above has a more prominent presence in the flavor profile. The complex combination of various elements explodes quickly on your palate, and spreads rapidly as well. It all evolves into a slightly tart tail that fits in well with the other aspects of this saké. Asahi Tenyū benefits from a bit of decanting.

Chilling this saké drowns out its special characteristics a bit too much; room temperature is fine, but gentle warming really enhances things. Not to be missed for kanzaké fans.

Kaishun
"Kome no Shizuku" • *junmaishu*
Shimane Prefecture

Nihonshu-do:	+5	Acidity:	1.6
Alcohol:	15 – 16%	Rice:	Gohyakumangoku
Semaibuai:	55%	Yeast:	Number 9

This place makes a very small amount of saké each year, something in the vicinity of five hundred koku, or about nine hundred kiloliters a year. Yet some truly outstanding saké comes from this kura. A mellow, soft, mature fragrance greets you, leading into a wide range of flavors blended together. A nice, high acidity supported by an underlying bitter trace allows the flavor to spread quite nicely over your palate.

OTHER OFFERINGS: This brewery's dainginjō is balanced and well defined. Distinct and lively, it is sure to please.

五 橋

Gokyō
Junmaishu
Yamaguchi Prefecture

Nihonshu-do:	+5	Acidity:	1.6
Alcohol:	15.5%	Rice:	Gohyakumangoku, Nihonbare
Semaibuai:	60%	Yeast:	Number 601

There is plenty to say about this saké. It is quite complex and chameleon-like: it seems to be slightly different on each occasion it is tasted. The fragrance alone is full of fruity scents that don't seem to stay still; it starts out as persimmon-like and melts into a touch of lemon. It initially hits the palate in a very dry way; little sweetness is evident on the tongue. It's light and delicate and seems full of flavors that blend well together. Yet in spite of all this, it is quite clean, devoid of any flavors that don't seem to belong. The first half of the flavor profile has an overall softness to it. The tail is slightly shibui, or tart-astringent, and a gentle nigami (bitterness) slowly raises its head just before the saké passes into your throat.

金 冠 黒 松 「錦 帯 橋」

Kinkan Kuromatsu
"Kintaikyō" • *tokubetsu honjōzō*
Yamaguchi Prefecture

Nihonshu-do:	±0	Acidity:	1.4
Alcohol:	15 – 16%	Rice:	Hattan, Nihonbare
Semaibuai:	60%	Yeast:	Number 601

The Kinkan Kuromatsu kura has won more gold prizes for new saké at competitions than any other kura in its prefecture. This particular saké is named after a famous bridge in the area.

The nose is faint, but has hints of slightly spicy green grapes, with just a touch of citrus. Light but full, with a very soft kuchiatari (sensation with which it strikes your palate) due to the soft water of the region. There is a nice fukarami spreading sensation throughout your mouth. It is slightly sweeter near the end than at the beginning, but then the kire (how it disappears from your palate) is quite quick. A good and solid ricelike sweetness hangs out for a while, making the tail long but not cloying. The acidity at the end seems to sustain this.

かほり鶴

Kahoritsuru
Junmaishu
Yamaguchi Prefecture

Nihonshu-do:	-0.5	Acidity:	1.9
Alcohol:	16.5%	Rice:	Akebono
Semaibuai:	60%	Yeast:	Number 7

Here is a gutsy saké from a small kura in Yamaguchi Prefecture. Kahoritsuru is everything a junmaishu should be — sturdy and balanced despite a relatively high acidity. The sharpness and high acid can also be found in the nose, but they are supported by other flavor elements and a great lack of *zatsumi*, or off-flavors. A very clean junmaishu. The nose has a touch of grapefruits and other citrus fruits. Great with food that has a strong garlic element. The tail sticks around a long time, which may not be to everyone's liking. Because of these qualities, this saké may be better with food than by itself.

屋久島

Yakushima
Tokubetsu junmaishu
Yamaguchi Prefecture

Nihonshu-do:	-0.5	Acidity:	1.5
Alcohol:	15 – 16%	Rice:	Yamada-Nishiki
Semaibuai:	50%	Yeast:	Number 9

The water source originally used to make this saké is no longer tapped due to the effects of industrialization. Therefore, water is brought to the kura by boat from a place called Yakushima in Kagoshima Prefecture (which has no saké breweries, by the way).

This water is incredibly soft, with a minimum of iron or calcium. The saké made from it is also incredibly soft. This is its overriding quality; it really melts deep into your palate almost instantly. Very unique. The flavor is not as sweet as the nihonshu-do suggests, but rather mildly so, and goes quite well with the other characteristics of this saké. Serve cool or chilled rather than warm.

あやきく「国重」

Ayakiku
"Kunishige" • *ginjōshu*
Kagawa Prefecture

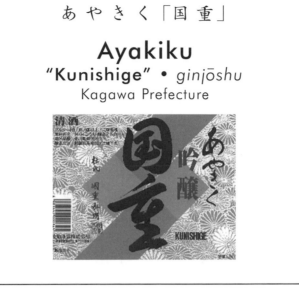

Nihonshu-do:	+5	Acidity:	1.2
Alcohol:	15.3%	Rice:	Ōseto
Semaibuai:	50 – 55%	Yeast:	Number 9

The name of this saké is the first name of the tōji of this kura. A light and crisp saké, Kunishige bears a thread of character that is particular to all Ayakiku saké. It's hard to describe, but it is almost a slight tanginess in the recesses of the flavor profile. Just try it.

OTHER OFFERINGS: Their daiginjō is a bit lighter, with a fruity nose, and comes in a beautiful box as well.

金 陵

Kinryō
Honjōzō
Kagawa Prefecture

Nihonshu-do:	+1.5	Acidity:	1.4
Alcohol:	15.7%	Rice:	Ōseto
Semaibuai:	58%	Yeast:	Kumamoto Yeast

The flavor of this saké is quite full and distinctive, especially for a honjōzō. It has some slightly sweet tendencies, but these are balanced well by some slightly bitter and earthy qualities that make this saké an excellent overall choice for warming. Whether warm or cold, all the flavor elements are connected somewhere on a deep level, producing a blended, balanced saké.

土佐鶴

Tosatsuru
Junmaishu
Kōchi Prefecture

Nihonshu-do:	+6	Acidity:	1.6
Alcohol:	15 – 16%	Rice:	Gohyakumangoku
Semaibuai:	65%	Yeast:	Kumamoto Yeast

Tosatsuru is a fairly large kura, definitely one of the larger in its region. Its name comes from the ancient name for this region, Tosa. The fragrance is low-key, with a slightly sweet and creamy touch to it. The flavor is dry and even, balanced, with no overwhelming aspect. It has the unique characteristic of being able to create esentially the same sensation everywhere on the palate, and sustain it for some duration.

A fairly long and tangy tail, with a high acid content that tickles the sides of your tongue. Room temperature or mild warming flatters this saké a bit.

OTHER OFFERINGS: Tosatsuru also makes a ginjō version of this junmaishu, and a bone-dry honjōzō that are both worth checking out.

酔 鯨

Suigei

Junmai ginjōshu
Kōchi Prefecture

Nihonshu-do:	+8	Acidity:	1.7
Alcohol:	16 – 17%	Rice:	Matsuyama Mitsui
Semaibuai:	50%	Yeast:	Number 901

Suigei is in some ways typical of the region known long ago as Tosa. A quick glance at the nihonshu-do and the acidity indicates that Suigei is dry and sharp. Although these parameters are not always indicative of what is to come, in this case they are quite telltale.

Suigei also seems to have a lot of body, and somehow gives the impression that it is heavier and fuller than it really is. A light amber color supports this. The nose is light and lively, more citric than anything else, and the tail is quick to make its exit.

司牡丹「船中八策」

Tsukasa Botan
"Senchū Hassaku" • *junmaishu*
Kōchi Prefecture

Nihonshu-do:	+8	Acidity:	1.4
Alcohol:	15 – 16%	Rice:	Yamada-Nishiki, Kita-Nishiki
Semaibuai:	60%	Yeast:	Number 9

The label on this saké, very easily recognized by its fluorescent orange color, says *chō karakuchi,* or superdry. Yet, unlike much saké made to be dry, they didn't throw out the baby with the bathwater here — a good amount of flavor and distinction remain.

The nose is slightly fruity, with an acidic touch. The flavor is indeed quite dry, but actually fairly soft, more so than the nose might indicate. The entire collection of flavors all melt on the tongue, leaving just a touch of their essence remaining. Good for warming, but also fine chilled. Be careful: this goes down all too easily.

梅錦「酒一筋」

Umenishiki
"Saké Hitosuji" • *junmaishu*
Ehime Prefecture

Nihonshu-do:	-2	*Acidity:*	1.9
Alcohol:	16.9%	*Rice:*	Yamada-Nishiki, Gohyakumangoku
Semaibuai:	55%, 60% respectively	*Yeast:*	Number 9

Ehime Prefecture has more kura than any prefecture on the island of Shikoku — over sixty. Yet, a great many of these are extremely small. Umenishiki, however, is one of the fifty biggest kura in Japan.

This saké has a gentle nose, barely discernible, but with a touch of cherries. It hits the palate lightly and spreads slowly. Dry throughout, with a dry and acidic finish that is subtly supported by a gentle fruitiness, this saké leaves a hearty essence in its wake.

鳴門鯛

Narutotai
Daiginjō
Tokushima Prefecture

Nihonshu-do:	+5	Acidity:	1.6
Alcohol:	16%	Rice:	Yamada-Nishiki
Semaibuai:	40%	Yeast:	MG

Dry and crisp, with a touch of bitterness that is quite nice, this saké is distinctive and unique. The nose is lighter and fruitier than the flavor would lead one to believe, and is quite pronounced. Narutotai would be nice slightly warmed as well as slightly chilled, with different characteristics appearing at varying temperatures. It's better at room temperature, with mellow-flavored food.

All of the kōji here is made by hand in kōjibuta trays. Special yeast, usually used for yamahai-shikomi, goes into most of the saké made here, giving it a slightly wild, looser taste profile.

繁 桝

Shigemasu
Junmai ginjōshu
Fukuoka Prefecture

Nihonshu-do:	+2	Acidity:	1.4
Alcohol:	15 – 16%	Rice:	Yamada-Nishiki, Reihō
Semaibuai:	50%	Yeast:	Number 9

A very satisfying brew, but hard to define. The nose is faint but really complex, with some acidity and a touch of spice. The flavor is somewhat spicy and dry, with a unique richness that draws your attention to it with every sip. Stable and solid, with a fairly low acid presence. The kire (how it disappears from your palate) is very nice, and it leaves a pleasant but hard-to-nail-down flavor.

A nice saké to drink chilled or at room temperature.

OTHER OFFERINGS: This kura also makes a wonderful daiginjō called Hako-iri Musume, or Girl in a Box, that's as tasty as its name is questionable. (This Japanese phrase refers to an overprotected and naive daughter.)

三井の寿「麗吟」

Mii no Kotobuki
"Reigin" • *ginjōshu*
Fukuoka Prefecture

Nihonshu-do:	+5	Acidity:	1.5
Alcohol:	15 – 16%	Rice:	Reihō
Semaibuai:	55%	Yeast:	Number 9

A crisp and short-lived fragrance with a touch of pine and flowers is a feature of this saké. Reigin is quite easy to drink, and goes well with a wide variety of food. It's wonderful when it warms up to room temperature. Dry but with a nice, fat presence and good substance. Light but not overly delicate, the flavor is both fruity and ricelike at the same time.

In order to get the flavor just where they want it, saké at this kura is stored for maturation and pasteurized in 1.8-liter bottles, returned to large tanks for blending and flavor assessment, then returned to bottles. A painstaking effort that definitely pays off.

東一

Azuma Ichi
Ginjōshu
Saga Prefecture

Nihonshu-do:	+5	Acidity:	1.4
Alcohol:	17%	Rice:	Yamada-Nishiki
Semaibuai:	40%	Yeast:	Kumamoto Number 9

Although the flavor of this saké is slightly on the dry side, the nose has a charm and personality all its own. The fragrance changes from sweet to slightly tart almost every time you taste it. There is a particular tartness that is distinctive and memorable. Good at room temperature.

OTHER OFFERINGS: Azumaichi's daiginjō is lively but mature, and a great complement to strong seafood dishes.

Mado no Ume
"Kaden" • ginjōshu
Saga Prefecture

Nihonshu-do:	+4	Acidity:	1.5
Alcohol:	15.5%	Rice:	(various)
Semaibuai:	50%	Yeast:	Number 9

A well-defined nose that is indicative of some citrus fruit, grapefruit perhaps, and something a bit more aged as well. The flavor of this saké is slightly dry, and also has a somewhat aged nuance to it. There are somewhat earthy facets to the flavor as well. Good slightly warmed but also fine when chilled.

Kōro
Junmai ginjōshu
Kumamoto Prefecture

Nihonshu-do:	+0.5	Acidity:	1.5
Alcohol:	16 – 17%	Rice:	Hattan-Nishiki
			Yamada-Nishiki
Seimaibuai:	52%	Yeast:	Number 9

Saké from Kyushu often has a heaviness, almost a distinctive boldness to the flavor. Somehow it seems reminiscent of the shōchū distilled liquor for which the island is famous. Generally dry, Kyushu saké has bitter and acidic elements that are a touch stronger than saké from other regions. In good saké from this region, all this is balanced and blended superbly.

Kōro, however, doesn't really fit this description of the typical Kyushu saké. It has a very full flavor that spreads through your mouth quickly, a quality known as *fukurami ga ii*. It's a fun saké — light, snappy, and sharp. The fragrance is also unique; it is slightly fruity, almost with a hint of strawberries. Kōro has its charms both chilled and warmed.

千代の園「朱盃マークⅡ」

Chiyo no Sono
"Shuhai Mark II" • *junmaishu*
Kumamoto Prefecture

Nihonshu-do:	+6	Acidity:	1.4
Alcohol:	15%	Rice:	Yamada-Nishiki
Semaibuai:	45%	Yeast:	Kumamoto Yeast

Chiyo no Sono is a deliciously typical example of a saké with a Kyushu feel. Solid, stable, and earthy, the bitter elements of the flavor profile are boldly prominent. There is a deliberateness about the taste of this saké, and its balance makes it even more memorable. Slight warming brings out a special charm. The fragrance, although delicate, has a bit of chocolate in it.

菊 の 城

Kiku no Shiro
Junmai ginjō
Kumamoto Prefecture

Nihonshu-do:	+2	Acidity:	1.5
Alcohol:	53%	Rice:	Yamada-Nishiki
			Reihō
Semaibuai:	53%	Yeast:	Kumamoto Yeast

Kiku no Shiro has a decidedly earthy quality to it, a mature and settled warmth created by the presence of a lot of little things. It is soft, full, and a bit heavier than average. The fragrance is suggestive of the flavor to come. With only a bit of imagination, it seems to have a thread of connection to shōchū, that distilled Kyushu specialty. This is not surprising, perhaps, considering that in Kumamoto Prefecture they make nihonshu in the northern half of the prefecture while in the southern half they focus their efforts on shōchū.

西 の 関

Nishinoseki
Junmaishu
Ōita Prefecture

Nihonshu-do:	-2	Acidity:	1.6
Alcohol:	15.7%	Rice:	Reihō
Semaibuai:	60%	Yeast:	Number 7

Nishinoseki is a distinctive and unique saké with a satisfying flavor overall. It comes into the palate with a soft and ever-so-slightly sweet flavor to it, and a pleasing bitter touch to the underlying flavor elements. There's a certain richness to the flavor, with a rare hint of cocoa. The tail disappears quickly, which just makes you want to taste it again. Nishinoseki is quite good at room temperature, but also has a special charm when warm.

CHAPTER EIGHT

ON COLLECTING SAKÉ LABELS

*J*ust because you've polished off a bottle of saké doesn't mean it's time to throw it out. The labels of saké bottles often have appealing designs, and collecting them can be fun. (It would be more fun if certain kura didn't insist on using cosmic-strength bonding glue.)

The names themselves are creative and evocative, and often even a bit humorous. As in many Japanese names for both people and places, nature is definitely an overriding theme, very often with a quite pleasing effect. But the readings of the kanji characters themselves are often cryptic and obscure, even to fairly literate people.

Not surprisingly, many saké names bear reference to the obsolete place-names of the regions in Japan from which they come. The best example is Niigata saké. The ancient name for this region is Echigō (越後), with an alternate reading for the character being *koshi*. With a few exceptions from neighboring Fukui Prefecture, you can safely bet that any saké beginning with the word Koshi is from Niigata Prefecture. Koshi no Kanbai is certainly the most famous, but there are many others including Koshi no Hakubai and Koshi no Homare.

Other examples of this include saké from Iwate Prefecture using the word Nanbu（南部）, and saké from Shimane Prefecture using the word Izumo（出雲）.

The interesting aspects of kanji characters used in saké names have not escaped the Japan Saké Brewers' Association. Somewhere deep in their offices sits someone with not enough to do. Having come to the conclusion that there were not enough curious statistics about the world of saké, this person counted the number of times various kanji characters were used in saké names. As of 1995, the results were: The most common character used in saké names is that for mountain （山）, whether it is read as *yama* or *san*, as in Otokoyama of Hokkaido or Gassan of Shimane Prefecture. The second most common character used in saké names is *tsuru*（鶴）, the character for crane

The next two characters on this list are almost always used together as *masamune*（正宗）, as in Sakura Masamune, from a large kura in Kobe (the first to use these characters to name a saké), as well as almost two hundred other sakés throughout Japan.

The next most common kanji character used is that for *kiku*（菊）, or chrysanthemum. Kikuhime from Ishikawa Prefecture is one excellent example, and Kiku Masamune, another large kura in Kobe, obviously strikes a resonant chord in many people, judging by how well their saké sells.

Despite the aforementioned tendency toward unusual readings of kanji characters when they are used in saké names, these names in general seem to have a predictable pattern, almost a rhythm to them. For example, the character 東 is almost always read *azuma* rather than *tō* or *higashi,* even though these are much more common readings. Two examples of the latter reading of this character are the saké Azuma Rikishi from Tochigi Prefecture and Azumaichi from Saga Prefecture.

Another example is the character 華, which means flower. This character is more often than not read as *hana* when used in saké names. Saké using this character reading often come from Hiroshima Prefecture, Hanahato being one, but Koshi no Hana from Niigata Prefecture is another example. This character reading has its exceptions, however. Sometimes the character is read as *ka*, as in Nihonka from Mie Prefecture.

Following the proclivity of marketing people in Japan to designate a day to remember their products, October 1 has been labeled *Saké no Hi,* or Saké Day. Although it may be pushing the envelope just a bit, the character 酒 closely resembles the character for saké (酉), and can be read *tori*, which is the tenth cycle on the Chinese zodiac calendar. Hence the selection of a day in the tenth month to be Saké Day.

These little gems of knowledge can go a long way in impressing your local shopkeeper or a drinking partner as they'll help you to read arcane saké labels on first sight. It can also make shopping a whole lot easier and more interesting.

PART THREE

その三
居酒屋と酒屋

CHAPTER NINE

SAKÉ PUBS AND RETAILERS OF GOOD SAKÉ

*J*apan is full of good saké pubs (*nomiya*); you just have to poke around. They can be found in just about any neighborhood, in all styles and price ranges. What is presented here is just a cross section of what's available. Most of the pubs are in Tokyo and its immediate environs; however, a few pubs in other areas of Japan are also listed.

There are also countless liquor shops that stock excellent saké. These often cater to a regular clientele that keeps them busy enough to escape the need to advertise or get too ambitious, so they may not be famous. Other shops stock hundreds of brands or put out newsletters or specialize in difficult-to-find brands and therefore are more high-profile. The latter kind of shop is typically mentioned in this chapter, but please keep in mind that there are innumerable small but wonderful saké shops around.

In addition, very often the shopkeeper may be clueless, but his *tonya-san* (wholesaler) may know saké well. This results in an average-looking shop that has several great brands of saké. It pays to check everywhere.

In terms of accessibility, large department stores in Japan just can't be beat. Most of these stock a wide range of all grades and types of saké. Any department store on a major train line is a sure bet for finding good saké. Quite often, local saké from smaller kura that cannot be easily found in major Japanese cities can be picked up at locations just a bit into the countryside (read: within an hour or so of a big city).

Most saké shops do not have English menus of English-speaking staff. Bring along a Japanese-speaking friend if you think you may have trouble making yourself understood.

SAKÉ PUBS IN TOKYO AND ENVIRONS

Below are recommended saké pubs (izakaya) in Tokyo, Yokohama, and Kanagawa, accompanied by area maps and short descriptions. They are listed in alphabetical order. This section is followed by a listing of a few select pubs in Hokkaido, Sendai, Nagoya, Kyoto, Osaka, Hyogo (near Kobe), and Fukuoka in Kyushu. I have not necessarily checked out all of the places in the latter category. If you want to be certain of what you'll find there, check with a knowledgeable local first.

WHAT THE SYMBOLS MEAN

¥ : Inexpensive (¥2500-¥3500)

¥¥ : Moderate (¥3500-¥5000)

¥¥¥ : Expensive (¥5000-¥6500)

¥¥¥¥ : Very Expensive (¥7000-¥12,000)

🍶 : 10 saké selections or less

🍶🍶 : 10-25 saké selections

🍶🍶🍶 : 25-100 saké selections

🍶🍶🍶🍶 : 100 saké selections or more

KEY TO THE MAPS

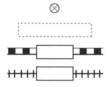

Police box

Subway station

JR line

Private railway line

味 吉

Ajiyoshi

Aijoshi boasts more types of saké than anyplace else in the Tokyo area: about 350, all listed on hanging strips of paper around the long counter. But this place has its quirky rules, also posted on the wall. They don't like to give recommendations on saké; No strong perfumes; Don't talk too much to the staff or those around you, and so on.

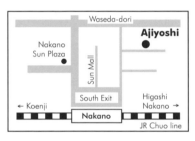

5-59-1 Nakano
Nakano-ku, Tokyo
☎ 03-3388-5471
Open Mon–Sat
6PM–1:30AM
Sun and holidays 6PM–1AM

赤 鬼

Akaoni

An excellent pub with many standard selections, as well as plenty of hard-to-find and seasonal offerings. Absolutely sterling saké at fair prices. Knowledgeable and serious but friendly staff. When it comes to blending saké and food, there are some real culinary treasures here. Reservations and the sashimi *moriawase* (selected sashimi) are both highly recommended.

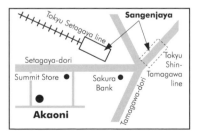

2-15-3 Sangenjaya
Setagaya-ku, Tokyo
☎ 03-3410-9918
Open 5:30–11:30PM
Sat 5–11:30PM
Closed Sun and holidays

天乃川

Amanogawa

The interior of this pub is an excellent example of Japanese design in a modern context. Mostly ginjōshu here. Feel free to leave yourself in the hands of the well-informed staff. Plenty of wonderful, classy selections. The *tsumami* (snacks) are tasty and well presented. Excellent choice for a light tasting session when there is no concern over the bill.

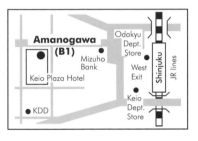

Keio Plaza Hotel, B1
2-2-1 Nishi Shinjuku
Shinjuku-ku, Tokyo
☎ 03-3344-0111 Ext 5950
Open daily
11:30AM–2PM (lunch),
5–10PM

あら川

Arakawa

The mainstay of this highly polished place is tempura, and it's top rate. The saké is extremely well chosen; the manager will enthusiastically drag you to the glass refrigerator to proudly show you his selections and make suggestions. Listening to this advice is heartily recommended.

Odakyū Mansion 1F
3-3-1 Higashi-Jūjō
Kita-ku, Tokyo
☎ 03-3912-1430
Open 11:30AM–2 (lunch),
5PM–9
Closed Wed

備 長

Binchō

A dark and woody interior. Excellent yakitori, with both the chicken and the coals being brought in from distant prefectures. Your best bet is the ¥3,500 course; it's filling and tasty. There's plenty of good saké to choose from, but beware the menu — it's a chore. Unless you read artistically cursive Japanese well, point or ask for your saké.

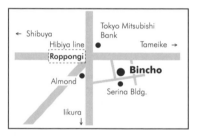

Marina Bldg. 2F
3-10-5 Roppongi
Minato-ku, Tokyo
☎ 03-5474-0755
Open daily 6PM–12AM

知 花

Chihana

Very creative, even funky food, but always fresh and tasty. Located a five-minute walk from Tokyo Station. A modern Japanese interior, with one large communal table and several low-tabled *zashiki* surrounding that. A wide range of other beverages too, like wine, shōchū, and awamori from Okinawa. And get this: a saké menu in English!

1-7-10 Yaesu
Chiyoda-ku, Tokyo
☎ 03-3245-1666
Open Mon–Fri 5:30–11PM,
Sat 4–10PM
Closed Sun and
national holidays

呑者家

Donjaka

The place to be if you missed the last train in Shinjuku. Eyebrow-raising yet simple variations on Japanese food that are worth a try. A modern, lighter atmosphere than the average saké pub. Good, solid workingman's saké is more common here than ginjōshu.

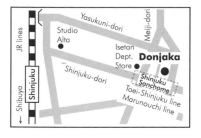

Fujidō Bldg 2F
3-6-12 Shinjuku
Shinjuku-ku, Tokyo
☎ 03-3357-8090
Open daily 4PM–5AM

フーズバー

Foods Bar

Quiet, in spite of its location just off of the raucous road to Roppongi. A woody interior with about 15 carefully selected sakés from around Japan, and good food. Just a wide enough variety of saké to allow proper perusing without becoming overwhelmed by the options.

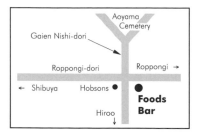

Nihon Kōtsū Anzen Kyōiku
Center 2F
3-24-20 Nishi Azabu
Minato-ku, Tokyo
☎ 03-3423-8140
Open Mon–Sat 6PM–2AM
Closed Sun

ふ　く　べ

Fukube

A real find. Fukube has been around since 1939, and the shop interior manages to maintain an old Tokyo integrity that only time can impart. Almost no ginjôshu, but forty or so excellent choices that include both warm and cool sakés. The food is mostly nibbles, nothing huge. Fukube is small, and calls for a touch of courtesy, although it is by no means boring or sedate.

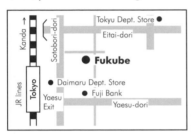

1-4-5 Yaesu
Chuo-ku, Tokyo
☎ 03-3271-6065
Open Mon–Sat
4:30–10:30PM
Closed Sun and holidays

玄　海　灘

Genkainada

This place is a gem. Upon entering, it looks like a normal Kyushu-style ramen shop, with an oval counter, and seats for less than 20 customers. But, lo and behold, there is a nihonshu menu! Just over 20 selections, and all of them excellent. Note the whiteboard on the wall: yakitori, salad, baked fish, and even sushi and sashimi from the sister shop upstairs are available.

3-2 Kanda Ogawamachi
Chiyoda-ku, Tokyo
☎ 03-3291-0053
Open Mon–Sat 5PM–12AM
Closed Sun and holidays

花 た ろ う

Hanatarō

¥¥¥¥
★★★★

Great atmosphere, excellent food, and excellent saké. Regardless of how much you eat and drink, the bill almost always seems to be ¥10,000. The best thing to do is to kick back and leave the saké selections to the manager. Make reservations. There is a happy-hour special of two cups of saké and two appetizers for a significantly lower price from 5 to 7PM.

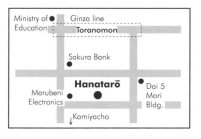

1-16-9 Toranomon
Minato-ku, Tokyo
☎ 03-3591-8970
Open Mon–Fri 5–11:30PM
Closed Sat, Sun and
holidays

は る ば る 亭

Harubaru Tei

¥¥
★★★

The one horseshoe-shaped counter surrounding the kitchen here is almost always full. This place has a small, devoted clientele that's younger and more hip than the average saké-drinking crowd. The tiny saké refrigerators in the corners are overflowing with selections. Seasonal vegetables are big on the menu here.

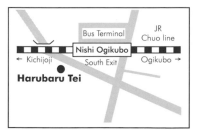

3-40-10 Shōan
Suginami-ku, Tokyo
☎ 03-3334-5133
Open 6PM–1AM
Closed Mon

壹
Ichi

A pleasant, calming atmosphere makes Ichi a good place for long, lingering meals. There are usually about fifteen or so saké selections, served in open vessels. Plenty to last the evening. The food consists of upscale and creative variations of traditional izakaya (pub-style restaurant) fare. Reservations recommended.

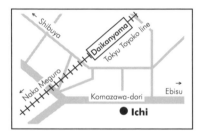

3-5-8 Ebisu Minami
Shibuya-ku, Tokyo
☎ 03-3715-0291
Open Mon-Sat
5:30–11:30PM
Closed Sun and holidays

いそむら
Isomura

Run by a friendly couple named (surprise) Isomura, this place has a really down-home feeling. It's quite small, accomodating no more than 20 customer. About 20 kinds of saké, and about 25 dishes that change daily with the season are scrawled upon a chalkboard for all to see.

Jūgō Bldg 2F
4-18-6 Shinbashi
Minato-ku, Tokyo
☎ 03-3433-3892
Open 5–11PM
Closed Sat, Sun, and
holidays

じゃぽん亭

Japontei

An eclectic shop with an appealing atmosphere that's stylish, modern, and artistic. The various saké cups are particularly diverse and attractive. Regulars here come in all ages, genders, and occupations. The food is mostly Japanese, with lots of fish, all presented very well. More of a shop for tasting various kinds of saké than a venue for heavy consumption.

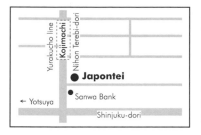

3-4 Kojimachi
Chiyoda-ku, Tokyo
☎ 03-3263-3642
Open Mon–Fri
11:30AM–3:30PM (lunch),
6PM–2AM
Closed Sat, Sun, and
national holidays

地酒

Jizaké

Jizaké stocks about 50 labels at any one time, and shakes up the offerings once or twice a year. For the most part, they sell saké by the 1.8-liter bottle, and if you are in a thirsty group, this is an inexpensive way to go. The cuisine is mostly fish, *nabe* (Japanese-style stew), and other small dishes designed to complement nihonshu.

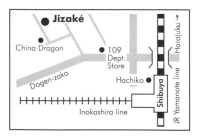

2-19-3 Dogenzaka
Shibuya-ku, Tokyo
☎ 03-3496-5295
Open Mon–Sat 5PM–3AM
Closed Sun and national
holidays

地 酒 屋

Jizaké-ya

A small shop with one tiny table and a counter that has a capacity of about 25 people. About 150 saké selections of all types and price ranges. Simple but decent food that, like the saké, is reasonably priced. The pleasant staff is generally busy, so don't expect to be coddled.

Dai-san Hirasawa Building 1F
2-46-7 Kabuki-chō
Shinjuku-ku, Tokyo
☎ 03-3205-3690
Open 6PM–1AM
Closed on the second Sun
of each month

十 徳

Juttoku

Very conveniently located (as is another branch, in Shibuya), with a spacious interior that rides a fine line between modern and traditional. Whiners would likely refer to this interior as incongruous, but no matter, a decent selection of great saké, tasty and varied food, and very good prices make this place fun and popular. They are big, too, on saké education.

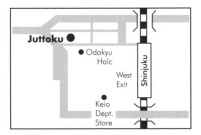

New Central Building B1, B2
1-15-12 Nishi Shinjuku
Shinjuku-ku, Tokyo
☎ 03-3342-0339
Open 4PM–12AM
Closed Sun

神 田 小 町

Kanda Komachi

Small, simple, homey saké pub in the center of the businessman's drinking headquarters of Tokyo. Although English will not get you very far, initial ordering from the diverse menu of saké and food is simplified by the availability of the "*kiki-zake* set," a 3-saké sampler, and the "*itamae* special," a 3-item nibbler. Usually packed, so arrive early.

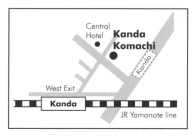

2-33-2 Uchi Kanda
Chiyoda-ku, Tokyo
☎ 03-3254-0025
Open 5–11PM
Closed Sun, holidays, and
the first and third Sat of
each month.

和 八

Kazuya

The fine yakitori, exploding with rich flavors, alone makes Kazuya worth the 3-minute train ride out of the Yamanote circle line loop. To add to this there are about 80 fine and reasonably priced saké. The manager has an intimate knowledge of the saké on offer; don't hesitate to ask for a recommendation.

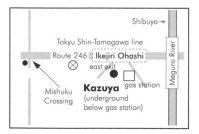

3-2-4 Higashiyama
Meguro-ku, Tokyo
☎ 03-5722-3321
Open every day 5PM–1AM

駒 八

Komahachi

Located in an unlikely neighborhood for such a place, Komahachi is no secret. It's always crowded and always fun. An interesting approach to food and large portions add to the experience. The manager is friendly and fun-loving, and roams among the patrons throughout the evening. About 20 good saké selections with plenty of information on each one.

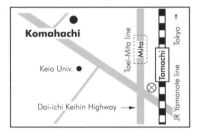

5-16-1 Shiba
Minato-ku, Tokyo
☎ 03-3453-2530
Open 5–11:30PM
Closed Sun and holidays

梢

Kozue

Kozue means "treetops," which is appropriate as Kozue sits on the forty-first floor of the Park Hyatt Tokyo and provides an unparalleled view of the city. Exquisite food and excellent saké, all in gorgeous presentation. Very modern and serene atmosphere, well-informed and attentive service. Best enjoyed on an expense account.

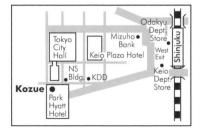

Park Hyatt Hotel, 41F
3-7-1-2 Nishi-Shinjuku
Shinjuku-ku, Tokyo
☎ 03-5323-3472
Open 11:30AM–2:30PM
(lunch),
5:30–10PM (dinner)

倉
Kura

Although the focus here is not really saké, but rather "creative food from all countries," there are a decent number of good saké to taste and explore. Much of the food goes very well with the nihonshu, which is served in interesting vessels. There are several branches of Kura around Tokyo.

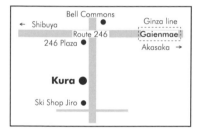

3-2-3 Minami Aoyama
Minato-ku, Tokyo
☎ 03-5474-0445
Open 5PM–2AM
Closed Sun and holidays

庫 裏
Kuri

A tiny saké pub for the true saké connoisseur. Run by the Kurihara family that runs the excellent saké retail shop across the narrow lane. You can sample from dozens and dozens of saké, and in varying glass sizes, making even the most expensive saké affordable in the right dosage. Note: no food except tiny snacks is served.

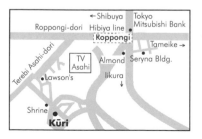

2-11-1 Moto Azabu,
Minato-ku, Tokyo
☎ 03-3497-0881
Open Mon–Sat 6–10:30PM
Closed Sun and national holidays

串 駒

Kushikoma

Extremely creative food, and the fish couldn't be any fresher. The manager is enthusiastic and unique, and his love for what he does is reflected in the food, drink, and atmosphere of the shop. Make reservations well in advance; it's small and popular.

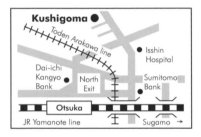

2-32-25 Kita-Ōtsuka
Toshima-ku, Tokyo
☎ 03-3917-6657
Open daily 6PM–12:00AM
Closed Sun

三 春 駒

Miharukoma

An excellent selection of saké on a well-organized menu. There is also a board on the wall that lists the most popular 20 selections in the pub, and since hundreds of customers can't be too far off, these are a safe bet. The regular menu is supplemented by seasonal selections on a chalkboard.

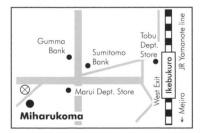

First Building
3-29-11 Nishi Ikebukuro
Toshima-ku, Tokyo
☎ 03-3971-0888
Open daily 5–11PM

もきち

Mokichi

Mokichi is recommended for a night of good, hearty *inaka* (countryside) food and saké to go with it. There are about 15 hearty saké here, with more coming from Yamagata than any other prefecture. There's plenty to taste, in a fun but decidedly not serene atmosphere. Come in a sociable mood.

Yokoderamachi 35
Shinjuku-ku, Tokyo
☎ 03-3267-5307
Open Mon–Sat
4:30–11:30PM
Closed Sun and holidays

夢 酒

Mushu

Located a good 10- to 15-minute walk from Otemachi Station, but only 30 seconds from Awajicho Station, also on the Marunouchi Line. This pub has a funky interior design with high-backed chairs, odd table shapes, and lighting that seems not altogether practical. Nevertheless, there's a wide and tasteful selection of saké served along with appealingly presented creative food.

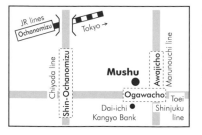

1-1-1 Kanda Awajicho
Chiyoda-ku, Tokyo
☎ 03-3255-1108
Open Mon–Sat 5–11:30PM
Closed Sun and holidays

なかむら

Nakamura

Dark, woody, modern, artistic, and romantic, Nakamura has atmosphere in spades. An excellent list of about twenty saké, with a few rather rare selections, and at fair prices. The food is outstanding with an appealing presentation. Everything is very fresh, with overall lively, unique flavors. Just a tad out of the way, but well worth that minor hassle.

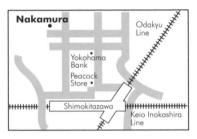

Shimokitazawa MT Building,
2F
2-37-3 Kitazawa
Setagaya-ku, Tokyo
☎ 03-3466-4020
Open daily 6PM–12AM
Closed Tues

大凧

Ōdako

Nothing beats hot *oden* (fish cakes and vegetables simmered in broth) in the winter, and nothing goes better with oden than saké. Over 2 rather small and cozy floors, Ōdako boasts about 45 kinds of saké. Several other non-oden side dishes that complement saké well are also available. Quiet jazz fills the spaces between the quiet conversations here.

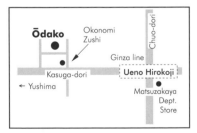

Sekine Bldg 1-2 floor
2-3-1 Ueno
Taito-ku, Tokyo
☎ 03-3836-4906
Open daily 5:30–10-30PM

大坂屋

Osaka-ya

Osaka-ya is a liquor shop running a *tachinomi* (a bar in which patrons must stand) on the side. Very narrow and cramped, so don't go with a crowd. Almost all the customers are fellows hailing from *shitamachi* stopping in for a quick cup. Quite a friendly crowd. There's a 2-drink limit.

2-2-2 Monzen Nakacho
Kōtō-ku, Tokyo
☎ 03-3641-2325
Open Mon–Fri 5–8:00PM
Closed Sat, Sun, and
holidays

龍馬

Ryūma

A large selection of both hard-to-find and commonly found saké is complemented by a curious menu that is built around 47 different *iwashi* (sardine) variations. There are also seasonal dishes that are not listed on the menu, so ask about these. Jovial manager; approachable staff.

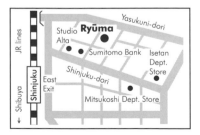

Dai-2 Sunpark Bldg. 3F
3-21-4 Shinjuku
Shinjuku-ku, Tokyo
☎ 03-3354-7956
Open daily 5PM–12AM

酒 菜 亭

Sakanatei

Although this small by cozy place seems well hidden, it is in fact well known, so make reservations. The food is creative and fresh, and much of it is displayed in bowls on the counter with little explanatory signs above. The saké is listed by type in the menu, complete with thorough descriptions. The staff is knowledgeable, friendly, and attentive.

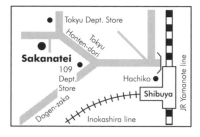

Koike Building 4th Floor
2-23-15 Dogenzaka
Shibuya-ku, Tokyo
☎ 03-3780-1313
Open Mon–Fri 5:30–11PM
(15:30–10:30PM on Sat)
Closed Sun

酒 の 穴

Saké no Ana

The location and the hours make Saké no Ana very user-friendly. The saké is divided on the menu by type, and there seems to be at least one saké from almost every prefecture in Japan. The food is traditional izakaya food, but perhaps a bit heavy on the tempura. The staff is prepared to give recommendations as well.

Ginza Rangetsu Building B1
3-5-8 Ginza
Chuo-ku, Tokyo
☎ 03-3567-1133
Open daily 11AM–11PM
Closed holidays

酒 の い け す

Saké no Ikesu

Quite a haul from downtown, but worth the trip once in a while, for both the food and drink as well as the ambiance. You can't miss this place: the *noren* curtain hanging outside (it indicates the shop is open) is brightly coloured, and empty saké casks are piled high out front. The manager is as clever and fun as he looks serious.

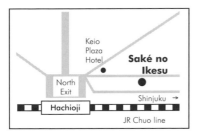

3-10-6 Meijin-chō
Hachioji-shi, Tokyo
☎ 0462-42-1508
Open Mon–Sat 5–11PM
Closed Sun and holidays

酒 ば や し ハ ン ナ

Sakébayashi Hanna

A quiet, friendly place 10 minutes from Roppongi crossing. It's real simple: all ginjōshu is ¥1,000 a glass, all junmaishu is ¥1,500 per decanter (more like a beaker), and all all honjōzō is ¥1,000 per decanter. All dishes are ¥500. Good, relaxed atmosphere.

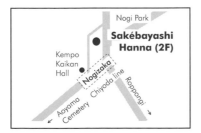

Sakébayashi Hanna 2F
1-25-2 Minami Aoyama
Minato-ku, Tokyo
☎ 03-3405-9888
Open Mon–Fri 6–11PM
Closed Sat, Sun and
holidays

さ く ら

Sakura

A charming and traditional shop. Reservations must be made at least two days in advance. The wonderful food is diverse, delicious, and has a real homemade touch. Courses start at ¥5,000, before the saké. You leave everything up to the manager; just give him a budget to work with (perhaps ¥10,000 to start).

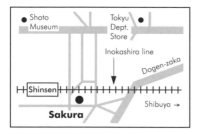

17-2 Maruyama-chō
Shibuya-ku, Tokyo
☎ 03-3461-2104
Open Mon–Sat
5:30–11:30PM
Closed Sun and holidays

笹 吟

Sasagin

Excellent food and a wide range of saké in an elegant, peaceful, and enjoyable setting. The proprietor balances polite aloofness with a very friendly willingness to help with saké and food selections. Considering the quality of the food, saké, and overall experience, this may be the best-valued saké pub in Tokyo.

1-32-15 Uehara
Shibuya-ku, Tokyo
☎ 03-5454-3715
Open Mon–Sat 5PM–12AM
Closed Sun and national holidays

笹 周

Sasashū

Sasashū has a warm atmosphere that's hard to beat especially for groups of four to six friends. The first floor, although a bit raucous, is in the center of the action and is generally more interesting. The tokkuri (saké flagons) come with little tags describing the ingredients, to help avoid confusion. Excellent grilled food.

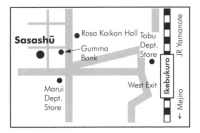

2-2-2 Ikebukuro
Toshima-ku, Tokyo
☎ 03-3971-9363
Open Mon–Sat 5–10PM
Closed Sun and holidays

春 秋

Shunjū

There are several branches of Shunjū, all worthy of a visit, but this one offers the best of atmosphere, decor, and saké. Elegantly dark and woody interior design. A well-chosen list of 20 saké or so, and high-class versions of simple country food like tofu, vegetables, and duck. And, at last visit anyway, an English menu.

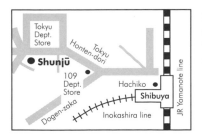

2-32-12 Dogenzaka
Shibuya-ku, Tokyo
☎ 03-3770-0019
Open daily 6–11:30PM

鈴 傳

Suzuden

Located in Toranomon, this atypical pub is boisterous and brightly lit. Not the place for a quiet evening. The food is the kind of stuff that can be served up quickly and inexpensively; it's not gourmet but it will fill you up. The saké is outstanding and very reasonably priced.

1-2-15 Toranomon
Minato-ku, Tokyo
☎ 03-3580-1944
Open Mon–Fri 5–10:30PM
Closed Sat, Sun, and holidays

立 花

Tachibana

A small, traditional shop in which only junmaishu is served. The yakitori, fish, and seasonal dishes are meant to complement junmaishu in particular. It adds up to excellent fare that goes well with nihonshu. The level-headed and friendly manager definitely knows his stuff.

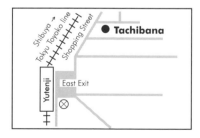

1-21-2 Yūtenji
Meguro-ku, Tokyo
☎ 03-3793-7434
Open Mon–Sat 5–11:30PM
Closed Sun and holidays

樽 一

Taruichi

Tucked away in the Kabukicho area of Shinjuku, Taruichi is eminently approachable. Whale, in all of its culinary manifestations, is the specialty of this establishment. With regard to saké, a great variety of Miyagi Prefecture offerings (the manager is from Miyagi) are available here. A good, wide selection of styles and grades.

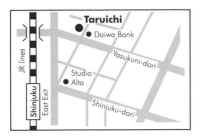

Dai-ichi Asagawa Bldg. 5F
1-17-12 Kabukicho
Shinjuku-ku, Tokyo
☎ 03-3208-9772
Open Mon–Sat 5-10PM
Closed Sun and holidays

友 廣

Tomohiro

Located just off Isezaki-chō mall near Kannai Station in Yokohama, this place has an excellent saké menu with a special section devoted to sakés from Niigata Prefecture, of which the manager is particularly fond. Fresh food, excellent sashimi in particular, and a master that greets and talks to the customers with unbridled enthusiasm are the hallmarks of this pub.

Fukutomi-cho Higashi-michi
38 Chuo-ku, Yokohama-shi
Kanagawa-ken
☎ 045-261-0078
Open Mon–Sat 5PM–2AM
Closed Sun and holidays

¥¥
★★★★

舍人庵

Tonerian

The more rustic first floor fills up quickly, so get there early if you want to be in the thick of things. The food here is more oriented to the season than most places. There's plenty of saké to choose from, with unique selections as well as more easily found brands.

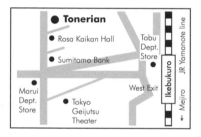

1-38-9 Nishi Ikebukuro
Toshima-ku, Tokyo
☎ 03-3985-0254
Open daily 4PM–12AM

¥¥¥
★★★

宇乃里

Unosato

A quiet, traditional shop within walking distance of Shibuya Station. Koto music plays in the background only steps from the frenzy of Tokyo. The food is delicate and beautifully presented, and the saké menu is just big enough to ensure there are both old favorites and new treats.

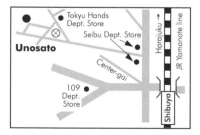

36-11 Udagawa-chō
Shibuya-ku, Tokyo
☎ 03-3496-2087
Open Mon–Sat 5–11PM
Closed Sun and holidays

やきとり雅

Yakitori Masa

Famous and lively, this shop has had its share of media exposure. The yakitori (skewered, grilled chicken and other meats) is tasty and reasonably priced. There is saké here to fit all budgets, from ¥600 a glass to ¥10,000 a glass, but there's no saké menu, so you must be able to recognize what you want and pick it out from the shelf.

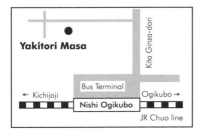

3-31-10 Nishi Ogi Kita
Suginami-ku, Tokyo
☎ 03-3395-9667
Open 5:30PM–12AM
Closed Wed

萬屋松風

Yorozuya Matsukaze

A dark and rustic shop that offers about 20–25 solid saké. The theme of the place is the folklore of the Hida Takayama region in Gifu Prefecture. The food is just the style you'd expect based on the rustic feeling of the place, and compliments the saké well.

1-24-5 Nishi Ikebukuro
Toshima-ku, Tokyo
☎ 03-3986-1047
Open Mon–Sat 5–11PM
Closed Sun and holidays

与っ太

Yotta

A small shop just off the beaten path. Excellent and diverse saké selections, some of which are permanent, while others change seasonally. The food has been well selected; the menu is diverse, and it all goes extremely well with nihonshu.

2-15-4 Asagaya Kita
Suginami-ku, Tokyo
☎ 03-3336-7650
Open Mon–Sat 6PM–12AM
Closed Sun and holidays

THE 坐

The Za

An excellent modern izakaya in the heart of Shibuya. Loud and boisterous. The food is excellent, wide-ranging, and creative. The crowd is varied enough that anyone can be comfortable here. The saké list is full of unique, zesty selections that are generally hard to get in Tokyo. The Za is fairly large, but it is also popular, so call ahead.

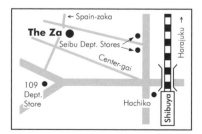

Nobara Bldg. 6F
25-9 Udagawa-cho
Shibuya-ku, Tokyo
☎ 03-3461-9598
Open daily 11:30AM–2PM
(lunch), 5PM–12AM

SAKÉ PUBS OUTSIDE TOKYO

◆ HOKKAIDO

Daikonya Shin-Nihon Ryōri
1-jō 6 chōme, Ai-no-sato, Kita-ku,
Sapporo-shi, Hokkaido
☎ 011-778-7180

Ginjō Tappore
Takase Bldg 1F, Minami 6-jō, Nishi 4 chōme
Chūo-ku, Sapporo-shi, Hokkaido
☎ 011-513-0534

Izakaya Den-Den
Number 7 Green Building, Minami 5-jō, Nishi 2 chōme
Chūo-ku, Sapporo-shi, Hokkaido
☎ 011-511-5141

Jizake Shot Bar Midori
Susukino Kaikan 1F, Minami 6-jō, Nishi 4 chōme
Chūo-ku, Sapporo-shi, Hokkaido
☎ 011-531-9280

◆ MIYAGI

Isshin
Daihatsu Bldg B1, 3-3-1 Kokubunchō
Aoba-ku, Sendai-shi, Miyagi-ken
☎ 022-261-9888

Sakabayashi
2-408 Ichibanchō, Aoba-ku,
Sendai-shi, Miyagi-ken
☎ 022-213-1758

◆ AICHI

Ginjō Taka
Taishō Seimei Bldg B1, 1-18-24 Nishiki
Chūo-ku, Nagoya-shi, Aichi-ken
☎ 052-203-8800

◆ KYOTO

Hira
Ichiban-kan B2, Nawate Shinbashi
Higashiyama-ku, Kyoto-shi, Kyoto
☎ 075-531-0863

Issei
Higashi Dōin East Entrance, Koro Dōri
Nishiki, Kyoto-shi, Kyoto
☎ 075-211-0824

◆ OSAKA

Aji Katsu
2-14-18 Miyako-chō Hori
Nishi-ku, Osaka-shi, Osaka
☎ 06-445-8103

Duo Yoshida
5-31 Shuyūeimoncho
Chūō-ku, Osaka-shi, Osaka
☎ 06-213-7145

Horikawa
4-4-7 Horie
Nishi-ku, Osaka-shi, Osaka
☎ 06-536-3050

Ja Fance
Sase Umeda Bldg B1, 1-1-27 Shibata
Kita-ku, Osaka-shi, Osaka
☎ 06-372-7667

Kawazu
1-1-3 Shibata
Kita-ku, Osaka-shi, Osaka
☎ 06-372-0820

Menbō Iwai
2-2-17 Imabashi, Imagawa Bldg
Chūō-ku, Osaka-shi, Osaka
☎ 06-222-4868

◆ HYOGO

Ginjō
1-7-3 Chōkyō Dōri, Chūō-ku,
Kobe-shi, Hyogo-ken
☎ 078-331-7840

Shunjū
2-11-13 Shimo Yamate-Dōri, Chūō-ku,
Kobe-shi, Hyogo-ken
☎ 078-331-1174

◆ FUKUOKA

Kaname
2-2-18, Kokura Kita-ku,
Kitakyushu-shi, Fukuoka-ken
☎ 093-551-5020

Mamaya
2-4-20 Minami Honchō, Hakata-ku,
Fukuoka-shi, Fukuoka-ken
☎ 092-591-2525

Taruya
Yamanouchi Park Avenue Bldg. B1, 1-5-19 Kajimachi
Kokura Kita-ku, Kitakyushu-shi, Fukuoka-ken
☎ 093-511-2426

Teppira
3-11-24 Hakata Eki Mae, Hakata-ku,
Fukuoka-shi, Fukuoka-ken
☎ 092-471-9244

SAKÉ RETAILERS IN TOKYO AND ENVIRONS

Knowing all about saké and what you want is fairly useless if you don't know where to find it. Developing a good relationship with one or more *sakaya*, or liquor shops, is an excellent idea. Keep in mind that shops stocking good saké are everywhere, tucked into little nooks and crannies of neighborhoods all over Japan. There is certainly one near you, wherever you are.

Japanese department stores are an excellent place to start. Their stock alone may be enough to keep any saké enthusiast happy for quite a while. Almost every large department store maintains a large, well-tended stock of nihonshu in its basement the food hall.

In Tokyo, all the department stores along the Yamanote circle line are excellent choices, including Seibu, Tokyu, Sogo, Isetan, Odakyu, and others. Although they may not always carry saké from smaller kura, you may be surprised at what is actually available. When you get a bit farther away from the larger cities, local department stores can also be good places for finding locally brewed selections.

Yet smaller shops that only sell saké have a special charm to them. Tiny retailers who have a passion for nihonshu abound, and really do permeate the whole country. Ask around. Below is a by no means comprehensive selection of these smaller specialty retailers organized alphabetically. Most liquor shops are in Tokyo, but a few special sources are also listed.

Harunoya
3-50-28 Higashi Nagatani, Kōnan-ku,
Yokohama-shi, Kanagawa-ken
☎ 045-822-8849

Hasegawa Sakéten
3-24-8 Kitasuna, Koto-ku, Tokyo
☎ 03-3644-1756

Hashiwaya Sakéten
2-14-8 Minami Yukitani, Ota-ku, Tokyo
☎ 03-3729-7622

Inoue Shōten
2-1-15 Zushi, Zushi-shi, Kanagawa-ken
☎ 0467-73-2573

Jizaké no Koyama Shōten
798-1 Sekido, Tama-shi, Tokyo
☎ 0423-75-7026

Kagataya
5-19-15 Koyama, Shinagawa-ku, Tokyo
☎ 03-3781-7005

Kakinuma
3-19-18 Shikahama, Adachi-ku, Tokyo
☎ 03-3899-3520

Kanda Izumiya
2-8 Kanda Ogawa-chō, Chiyoda-ku, Tokyo
☎ 03-3294-0201

Kasugaya
818-1 Abiko, Abiko-shi, Chiba-ken
☎ 0471-85-1911

Kōshūya Sakéten
5-1-5 Minami Nagasaki, Toshima-ku, Tokyo
☎ 03-3954-2757

Machidaya
1-49-12 Kamitakada, Nakano-ku, Tokyo
☎ 03-3389-4551

Mikawaya
1-23-16 Kyodo, Setagaya-ku, Tokyo
☎ 03-3420-3201

Minatoya
2-35-9 Wakabayashi, Setagaya-ku, Tokyo
☎ 03-3413-3718

Mitsuya
2-28-15 Nishi Ogikubo Minami, Suginami-ku, Tokyo
☎ 03-3334-7447

Sakaya Kurihara
1-4-6 Naruse, Machida-shi, Tokyo
☎ 0427-27-2655

Sakaya Kurihara (Tokyo)
3-6-17 Moto-Azabu, Minato-ku, Tokyo
☎ 03-3408-5378

Sekiya Sakéten
5-10-2 Ueno, Taito-ku, Tokyo
☎ 03-3841-8384

Shimada Shōten
3-5-1 Tachi-uiri-bori, Nishi-ku, Osaka
☎ 06-531-8119

Shimaya Sakéten
3-14-23 Mitsuwadai, Wakaba-ku, Chiba-shi, Chiba-ken
☎ 043-252-3251

Suzuden
1-10 Yotsuya, Shinjuku-ku, Tokyo
☎ 03-3351-1777/03-3353-8695

Toshiyuki
4-137 Kamezaki-chō, Handa-shi, Aichi-ken,
☎ 0569-28-0219
Fax: 0569-28-2710

Uguisudani Yorozuya
3-4-16 Negishi, Taito-ku, Tokyo
☎ 03-3873-8146

Yamada-ya
3-8-29 Yuki-no-Shita, Kamakura-shi, Kanagawa-ken
☎ 0467-22-0338

SAKÉ RETAILERS IN THE U.S.

◆ **CALIFORNIA**

Beltramo's Fine Wines and Spirits
1540 El Camino Real
Menlo Park, CA 94025
☎ (650) 325-2806

K&L Wine Merchants
3005 El Camino Real
Redwood City, CA 94061
☎ (650) 364-8544

K&L Wine Merchants
766 Harrison St.
San Francisco, CA 94107
☎ (415) 896-1734

Maruwa Foods
1737 Post
San Francisco, CA 94115
☎ (415) 563-1901

Mill Valley Market Wines and Spirits
12 Corte Madera Ave.
Mill Valley, CA 94941
☎ (415) 388-8466

Mitsuwa San Jose Store
675 Saratoga Ave.
San Jose, CA 95129
☎ (408) 255-6699

Nijiya Market
2121 W 182nd St.
Torrance, CA 92504
☎ (310) 366-7200

Uoki
1656 Post
San Francisco, CA 94115
☎ (415) 921-0514

The Wine House
2311 Cotner Ave.
W. Los Angeles, CA 90064
☎ (310) 479-3731

◆ COLORADO

The Boulder Wine Merchant
2690 Broadway
Boulder, CO 80304
☎ (303) 443-6761

West End Wine Shop
777c Pearl St.
Boulder, CO 80302
☎ (303) 245-7077

◆ HAWAII

Daiei
801 Kaheka St.
Honolulu, HI 96814
☎ (808) 973-4800

Marukai
2310 Kamehameha Hwy.
Honolulu, HI 96819
☎ (808) 845-5051

◆ MASSACHUSETTS

Blanchard's Inc., The Super Liquor Store
103 Harvard Ave.
Allston, MA 02134
☎ (617) 782-5588

◆ NEW JERSEY

Mitsuwa New Jersey Store
595 River Rd.
Edgewater, NJ 07020
☎ (201) 941-9113

Super Savers Liquors
888 Rt. 22 East
Somerville, NJ 08876
☎ 908-722-6700

◆ NEW YORK

Ambassador Wines
1020 2nd Ave.
New York, NY 10022
☎ (212) 421-5078

Beekman Liquors
500 Lexington Ave.
New York, NY, 10017
☎ (212) 838-6551

Garnet Wines and Liquors
929 Lexington Ave.
New York, NY 10021
☎ (212) 772-3211

Park Avenue Liquor Shop
292 Madison Ave.
New York, NY 10017
☎ (212) 685-2442

67 Wine and Spirits
179 Columbus Ave.
New York, NY 10023
☎ (212) 724-6767

Union Square Wines
33 Union Square West
New York, NY 10003
☎ (212) 675-8100

◆ OHIO

Jungle Jim's
5440 Dixie Hwy.
Fairfield, OH 45014
☎ (513) 829-1918

◆ TEXAS

Monticello Liquor
4855 N. Central
Dallas, TX 75205
☎ (214) 520-6618

Nippon Daido
11138 Westheimer Rd.
Houston, TX 77042
☎ (713) 785-0815

◆ WASHINGTON

Pike and Western Wine Shop
1934 Pike Place
Seattle, WA 98101
☎ (206) 441-1307

Uwajimaya
600 5th Ave. South
Seattle, Washington 98104
☎ (206) 624-6248

Uwajimaya
15555 NE 24th St.
Bellevue WA 98133
☎ (425) 747-9012

GLOSSARY

amakuchi 甘口
Saké that tastes sweeter than neutral.

amino-san アミノ酸
Amino acid.

aru-ten アル添
Saké to which brewer's alcohol has been added; non-junmaishu saké.

atsukan 熱燗
Piping hot saké.

daiginjōshu 大吟醸酒
Fermented rice saké polished under 50% at low temperature. This is the highest class of saké.

dekasegi 出稼ぎ
The practice of leaving one's home and traveling to a distant place for work.

fune 槽
A large box (usually wooden), used for pressing moromi and separating lees from the fresh saké.

genmai 玄米
Unpolished rice; brown rice.

ginjōshu 吟醸酒
Fermented rice saké polished under 60% at low temperature.

go-mi 五味

The five representative flavors that are sometimes used as a framework for assessing saké: sanmi 酸味 (acidity), amami 甘味 (sweetness), karami 辛味 (dryness or spicyness), shibumi 渋味 (astrigency or tartness), and nigami 苦味 (bittcrncss).

hi-ire 火入れ

The saké pasteurization process.

honjōzōshu 本醸造酒

Saké made from rice, *kōji,* water, and a little alcohol.

ichigō 一合

A measure usually considered to be one serving of saké, equal to approximately 180 milliliters, roughly one masu's worth of saké.

isshō 一升

A measure equal to 1.8 liters, or ten gō, roughly ten masu of saké.

isshōbin 一升瓶

A 1.8-liter bottle of saké.

itto 一斗

A measure equal to eighteen liters, or ten times the volume of isshō.

ittōbin 一斗瓶

An eighteen-liter bottle, equal in volume to ten isshōbin; freshly pressed saké is often allowed to settle in this kind of vessel.

jōmai 蒸米

Steamed rice; the rice-steaming procedure.

jōzō 醸造

The saké-pressing process.

junmaishu 純米酒

Saké made only from rice, kōji, and water. This is pure saké.

kakemai 掛米

Steamed rice which is added to the fermenting moromi.

kan (o-kan, kanzake) 燗（お燗、燗酒)
A general term for warmed saké.

kaori 香り
The smell or fragrance of a saké.

karakuchi 辛口
Saké that tastes drier than usual.

kasu 糟
The lees that remain after moromi has been pressed to give clear saké; the unfermented remains of the moromi.

kōbo 酵母
Yeast.

kōji 麹
Rice cultivated with kōjikin; used in every stage of saké production.

kōjikin 麹菌
A mold, the Latin name for which is *Aspergillus oryzae*, used in saké production to break down starches in steamed rice into fermentable sugars.

koku 酷
Originally a measure of rice equal to one thousand masu, or about 380 kilograms, for saké, a measure equal to one hundred isshōbin, or about 180 liters.

koshiki 甑
A large vat, traditionally wooden, in which rice for saké brewing is steamed.

kuchiatari 口当たり
The flavor and impression just as a saké hits the tongue and palate.

kura 蔵
A saké brewery.

kurabito 蔵人
A saké brewery worker(s).

kyūbetsu seido 級別制度
The obsolete (abandoned in April 1989) saké classification system assigning a tokkyū 特級 (top class), ikkyū 一級 (first class), or nikyū 二級 (second class) ranking, along with requisite tax increases to the price of a bottle of saké.

masu 升
A small wooden box traditionally used for measuring rice and drinking saké.

moromi 醪
The fermenting mixture of rice, kōji, yeast, and water.

moto 酛
Also known as shubo, the yeast starter. A mixture of rice, kōji, yeast, and water in which an extremely high concentration of yeast cells is cultivated. (See *shubo*.)

mushimai 蒸し米
The rice-steaming step of saké production. (See *jōmai*.)

namazaké 生酒
Unpasteurized saké.

nuka 糠
The talc-like powder that is the outer portion of polished rice kernels.

nurukan 温燗
Saké warmed to lukewarm temperatures.

roka 濾過
The saké filtering process, undertaken when saké has been sitting for 10 days.

sakagura 酒蔵
Another word used to refer to a saké brewery.

sakaya 酒屋
A liquor shop that sells saké.

sandan shikomi 三段仕込
The most widely applied method of adding rice, kōji, and water to the moromi, a three-stage process.

seibun 成分
The components or chemical makeup of something, here used in reference to either saké or rice.

seimai 精米
Rice polishing.

semaibuai 精米步合
The degree to which rice has been polished; this number, expressed as a percentage, refers to the amount of grain that remains after rice has been polished. For example, a 35% semaibuai means that the rice has been polished so that it is only 35% of its original size, and that 65% of it has been turned into nuka.

seimaiki 精米機
The machine used to polish rice for saké.

senmai 洗米
The rice-washing step in saké brewing.

shinpaku 芯白
The hard, white center comprised of starch found in good saké-brewing rice.

shinseki 浸漬
The rice-soaking step of the saké brewing process.

shubo 酒母
Yeast starter, also known as moto. This is a mixture of rice, kōji, and water with an extremely high concentration of yeast cells. (See *moto.*)

tokutei meishōshu 特定名称酒
A collective term referring to honjōzōshu 本醸造酒, junmaishu 純米酒, and ginjōshu 吟醸酒.

tōji 杜氏
The head brewer of a brewery.

yongōbin 四合瓶
A bottle holding 720 ml, or four gō.

INDEX